GUIDE TO THE FIRST LADIES

by
Frederick Lawrence Jackson

SANTA MONICA PRESS
P.O. Box 1076
Santa Monica, CA 90406-1076
Printed in the United States
All Rights Reserved

This book may not be reproduced
in whole or in part or in any
form or format without written
permission of the publisher

©1994 SANTA MONICA PRESS

Table of Contents

Martha Dandridge Custis Washington   7

Abigail Smith Adams   10

Martha Wayles Skelton Jefferson   14

Dolley Payne Todd Madison   17

Elizabeth Kortright Monroe   21

Louisa Catherine Johnson Adams   24

Rachel Donelson Jackson   28

Hannah Hoes Van Buren   30

Anna Tuthill Symmes Harrison   31

Letitia Christian Tyler   35

Julia Gardiner Tyler   37

Sarah Childress Polk   40

Margaret Mackall Smith Taylor   43

Abigail Powers Fillmore   45

Jane Means Appleton Pierce	48
Mary Todd Lincoln	51
Eliza McCardle Johnson	55
Julia Dent Grant	58
Lucy Ware Webb Hayes	61
Lucretia Rudolph Garfield	64
Ellen Lewis Herndon Arthur	66
Frances Folsom Cleveland	68
Caroline Lavinia Scott Harrison	71
Ida Saxton McKinley	73
Edith Kermit Carow Roosevelt	75
Helen Herron Taft	78
Ellen Louise Axson Wilson	82
Edith Bolling Galt Wilson	84
Florence Kling Harding	88

Grace Anna Goodhue Coolidge	91
Lou Henry Hoover	93
Anna Eleanor Roosevelt Roosevelt	96
Elizabeth (Bess) Virginia Wallace Truman	99
Mamie Geneva Doud Eisenhower	102
Jacqueline Lee Bouvier Kennedy Onassis	104
Claudia Taylor (Lady Bird) Johnson	107
Thelma Catherine (Patricia) Ryan Nixon	110
Elizabeth Bloomer Ford	114
Rosalynn Smith Carter	117
Nancy Davis Reagan	120
Barbara Pierce Bush	122
Hillary Rodham Clinton	125

Martha Dandridge Custis Washington
Born: June 21, 1731
Died: May 22, 1802
First Lady: 1789-1797

Our nation's first First Lady was born in New Kent County, Virginia on June 21, 1731. The oldest of eight children of Colonel John Dandridge and Frances Jones Dandridge, young Martha was poorly educated, a handicap that is plainly illustrated in her few surviving letters. One such letter, written in 1758, includes instructions for the care of a nightgown: "... I have sent a night gound to be dide of an fashonob Corler fitt for me to ware and beg you would have it dide better that I sent Las year that was very badly don this gound is of a good Lenght for me."

Martha made up for her lack of education, however, with her sewing, weaving, and knitting skills, as well as her accomplishments as a horsewoman. Additionally, Martha's impressive common sense and excellent social graces prepared her for her later job as the First Lady of the United States.

When Martha turned 18, she married her Godfather, Daniel Parke Custis, who was some 20 years older than she. Their successful and happy marriage was cut short only eight years later on July 8, 1757, when Daniel died of heart failure. Upon his death, Martha inherited a substantial estate which included nearly 20,000 acres of rich tobacco land, nearly 200 slaves, their plantation home (ironically dubbed "The White House"), and close to 30,000 British pounds sterling. Together, Martha and Daniel had four children together, two of whom died in early childhood.

On March 16, 1758, George Washington, a young man with great ambitions but short on funds, was introduced to Martha while the two of them were visiting Colonel and Mrs. Richard Chamberlayne at their home in Poplar Grove. The short, rather plump Martha was no great beauty, but George apparently found her lovely hazel eyes warm and calming. Ten days later, the smitten Washington proposed to Martha at her estate. They were married the following January at an extraordinarily beautiful affair held at Martha's estate. George wore the blue uniform of his regiment, while Martha wore a silk dress. After a three month honeymoon at Martha's Williamsburg home, "Six Chimneys," the newlyweds settled down at Mount Vernon.

While George and the woman known as "The Mother of Our Country" did not have any children of their own, George raised Martha's son and daughter as if they were his own. Martha's early years at Mount Vernon were marked by her fondness for riding horses, playing the harpsichord, and singing. It was during this time that Martha developed a reputation for being a gracious hostess and a wonderful cook. In the meantime, George, with the help of Martha's considerable fortune, became an extremely successful tobacco farmer and landowner.

During the long years of the American Revolution, Martha often traveled to be at her husband's side. Carrying provisions from her home, she would make the precarious journey from Mount Vernon to Valley Forge and feed, clothe, and help heal the sick and wounded soldiers. Indeed, she was her husband's strongest supporter throughout the roller coaster years of the Revolution.

Shortly after George was elected President, Martha moved to New York, where the first capital of the United States had been established. The following year the couple moved to 190 High Street in the nation's new capital of Philadelphia; Martha and George did not live at the White House or in Washington D.C. at any time during his presidency.

Martha's rather undistinguished stint as First Lady was highlighted by her tradition of holding Friday evening receptions, which, if truth be known, were rather dull affairs. The first First Lady also had an effect on the fashions of the time, as her penchant for lace caps and bonnets, along with handkerchiefs around her neck, caught on with the populace.

On May 22, 1802, approximately two and a half years after her husband had passed away, Martha died of a high fever after suffering through 17 days of illness. She had spent her final years in relative seclusion, living in a small attic room. In her will, she ordered that all of the slaves at Mount Vernon be freed. She and her husband are buried next to each other in a vault at Mount Vernon.

Abigail Smith Adams

Born: November 22, 1744
Died: October 28, 1818
First Lady: 1797-1801

Unlike Martha Washington, Abigail Adams received a solid education, courtesy of her minister father, William Smith, and her maternal grandparents, Colonel John Quincy and his wife, Elizabeth. A voracious reader (she especially enjoyed Shakespeare and Moliere) and letter writer, Abigail had free reign of her grandparent's enormous home library, and even managed to teach herself French.

When Abigail, or "Abby" to her friends,

turned 15 she met a young lawyer named John Adams. Their courtship would last for five years, during which time they wrote to each other nearly every day. Abigail's mother was not too happy about her daughter's choice of a boyfriend. While John Adams had been educated at Harvard, he was not from a distinguished family, and consequently was not very wealthy. However, Abigail and John were deeply in love, and after years of invocation, Abigail's mother finally agreed to the marriage, and they were wed on October 25, 1764.

Together, Abigail and John would have five children, and Abigail somehow managed to retain her lovely figure in spite of her many pregnancies. Four of the five children would live reasonably long lives, but one, Susannah, would die soon after her first birthday. Sons John Quincy and Thomas would have distinguished careers, the former as the sixth President of the United States, the latter as the Chief Justice of the Massachusetts Supreme Court.

After spending the early years of their marriage in Braintree, Massachusetts, the couple moved their family to Boston, where John became a vocal advocate of independence for the country. Abigail stood behind her husband 100%, and when he went off to Philadelphia for the Continental Congress, Abigail began writing letters that are now regarded as classic records of the Revolutionary period. Her intelligence and insight contributed to fascinating reports on the political climate of the era. It should be noted that Abigail was even an early supporter of women's rights.

In 1784, after six long years of separation, Abigail joined her husband in Europe, where he had been working as a diplomat for our new and struggling country. When John was appointed as the first American ambassador to Britain in 1785, the couple moved to London. The years spent in Europe were not always happy ones for Abigail. While she certainly enjoyed many aspects of such cities as London and Paris, and while she also looked forward to entertaining the interesting people they were constantly meeting, she was often homesick for her friends and family on the other side of the Atlantic. Fortunately, John gave up his post and returned with Abigail to America in 1788. When he was elected Vice President in 1789, the couple moved to Philadelphia.

While the Adams's vice presidential years were relatively uneventful — John himself referred to the vice presidency as "the most insignificant office" that was ever created by man — John's term as our nation's President was an extremely rocky one for both him and his wife. The problems began, for Abigail anyway, with John's inauguration. Tending to her ill mother-in-law, Abigail was unable to attend the grand ceremony, and would not even join him in Philadelphia until several months into his presidency.

Her husband's term in office was marked by a great deal of criticism from both the public and the newspapers of the day. Critics often referred to Abigail as "Mrs. President," expressing the common belief that she held tremendous influence over her husband. Abigail's intense support of the Alien and Sedition Acts of 1798, which apparently led John to support the act as well, was overwhelmingly unpopular, and had a great deal to do with her husband's failure to win reelection in 1801.

When Abigail and John moved to the new Executive Mansion in Washington City, they were greeted by a town that was still in the process of being built. Roads were unfinished, and buildings were few and far between. Worse yet, their new home in what would eventually be called the White House, was practically uninhabitable. Drafty and damp, they had to keep fires burning all the time to stay warm, and had to live with very few conveniences. In fact, Abigail hung her laundry in the formal East Room because, legend has it, with two fireplaces it was the warmest room in the house!

When John was defeated in his bid for

reelection, the couple moved to Peacefield, Massachusetts. They spent 17 quiet years there, the high point of which was undoubtedly seeing their son, John Quincy, appointed Secretary of State. Unfortunately, these years saw Abigail constantly battling rheumatism and even St. Anthony's Fire (a severe skin condition). In October of 1818, Abigail suffered a stroke and passed away. She was buried in Quincy, Massachusetts. When John Quincy Adams was elected as the sixth President of the United States some seven years after his mother's death, Abigail became the only woman to have been both a wife and a mother of Presidents.

Martha Wayles Skelton Jefferson
Born: October 30, 1748
Died: September 6, 1782
First Lady: Died before husband took office

While Martha Jefferson was not officially a First Lady — she died some 18 years before her husband was elected as our third President — it is impossible to ignore the influence she had on one of our greatest leaders.

Martha was born in Charles City County,

Virginia to John Wayles, a lawyer and land owner, and Martha Eppes. Her mother died when she was very young, and her father remarried soon after. While no portrait of Martha survives, it was said that she was very beautiful, with large brown eyes and stunning auburn hair.

In 1766, when Martha was 18, she married Bathurst Skelton, whose brother had once been wed to the last of Martha's father's three wives. (Try to work out the genealogy of that relationship!!) Martha and Bathurst had a son within the first year of their marriage, but Bathurst died soon after, and her son would not live past the age of four.

A couple of years later, Martha met Thomas Jefferson, and their love began to bloom. They shared a passion for music — she was an accomplished musician, a fan of the harpsichord, and he played the violin and cello. They were eventually married on New Year's Day, 1772.

During the first year or two of their marriage, Thomas's political activity fell off, and he spent his time enjoying life with Martha. By all accounts, their marriage was an ecstatically happy one. After the birth of their second daughter, Jane, Jefferson returned to politics. However, Jane would live for only a year and a half, and during a recess of the Continental

Congress, Thomas returned home just in time to share, with Martha, the horrifying experience of watching their baby daughter die.

Sorrow hit Martha and Thomas again two years later when their first son died only three weeks after being born. Another daughter, Mary, was born on August 1, 1778. Mary and their first daughter, Patsy, would be the only Jefferson children to reach adulthood.

In 1781, the couple's fourth daughter died at the age of six months when the family was forced to flee Monticello in order to escape invading British troops. A distraught Thomas handed in his resignation as Governor and promised Martha that he would give up politics, a promise he kept while she was alive.

By the time Martha gave birth to their fifth daughter, the wife of our nation's future third President was gravely ill. Seven children in less than fourteen years had wreaked havoc on her delicate constitution. For the next four months, Martha remained in bed, with Thomas by her side. When she passed away in September of 1782, Thomas was devastated. He swore that he would never marry again, and he never did. Theirs was truly a love that was cut much, much too short.

Dolley Payne Todd Madison

Born: May 20, 1768
Died: July 12, 1849
First Lady: 1809-1817

One of the most popular First Ladies of all time, Dolley Madison was born in North Carolina and raised in Virginia. When she was 15 years old, her wealthy father freed his slaves, sold his plantation, and moved his wife and children to Philadelphia. Dolley's mother, Mary, was a strict Quaker, and Dolley was forced to wear dull gray clothes as a child — a practice she would rebel against with great style as an adult.

In 1789, her father's business failed and he was dismissed from the Quakers for being a debtor. Disgraced, he retreated to his bedroom, where he remained until his death three years later. During this period of crisis, Dolley met a young lawyer named John Todd. When John Todd asked Dolley to be his wife in 1790, she gladly accepted. They had two sons, John Payne and William Temple. Unfortunately, their marriage would not be a long one; three years later, when yellow fever descended upon Philadelphia, the epidemic took both Dolley's husband and her youngest child, William.

The 25-year-old widow was soon attracting

a crowd of suitors. One of these was "the great little Madison," a short, 43-year-old Congressman from Virginia. Urged by her friend Aaron Burr (then a New York Senator) and her distant cousin Martha Washington to accept the Congressman's proposal of marriage, Dolley consented, and the two of them were wed a mere five months after they had met.

Because James Madison was not a Quaker, Dolley was immediately thrown out of the Society of Friends. This had a liberating effect on Dolley, however, as she was now able to indulge in her hidden passion for fine clothing and jewelry, and entertain the most distinguished citizens of Philadelphia with great flash and flair.

When James retired from Congress in 1797, he and Dolley and her son moved to Virginia, where they spent a quiet four years. Their peaceful way of life at "Montpelier" was broken, however, when Thomas Jefferson appointed Madison as the Secretary of State and the family was on the move once again, this time to the still relatively new capital of Washington D.C. Because Jefferson was a widower (ditto for his Vice President, Aaron Burr), the President often asked Dolley to be the hostess at important affairs. On the political side, it should be noted that Dolley helped to raise funds for the Lewis and Clark expedition.

In 1809, Madison became the fourth President of the United States. On March 4th, Dolley became the first First Lady to witness her husband's inauguration, and later that evening she threw the first inaugural ball. Her clothes that night were truly fit for a Queen — a pale, buff-colored velvet gown accessorized with a gorgeous string of pearls, earrings and bracelets. On top of her head she wore a white satin head dress with two bird of paradise feathers. The turban would become her fashion trademark, a style that women across the country sought to imitate throughout her tenure as First Lady.

The early years of the Madison's stay at the White House were marked by a great deal of entertaining. Dolley instituted the first Easter Egg Roll for the children in Washington D.C., and she attended the first wedding ever held at the White House when her sister married a Supreme Court Associate Justice.

Trouble occurred, however, during the War of 1812. In August of 1814, British troops stormed the city. With Madison out with his troops, Dolley was left in charge of the original copies of the Constitution, the Declaration of Independence, and other important documents. When the British approached the White House she fled, saving these important historical items (not to mention a portrait of George Washington). When Dolley and James returned, they found the city in ruins and the White House practically burned to the ground. James wanted to relocate the capital to Philadelphia, but Dolley persuaded him to rebuild it in Washington D.C.

When Madison wrapped up his second term in office, the couple retired to "Montpelier," their estate in Virginia. They would spend the next 20 years entertaining guests, with Dolley still the grandest hostess of them all. James passed away on June 28, 1836, and Dolley was soon to discover that their funds were exceedingly low. James had lent Dolley's wayward son some $40,000 over the years, leaving Dolley virtually penniless.

But the resourceful Dolley gathered together Madison's papers and sold them to the Government for $30,000. She then moved back to Washington D.C., where she once again established herself as the preeminent hostess in the city. She continued to entertain for the next dozen or so years until her death on July 12, 1849. Her funeral, as befits someone like Dolley, was perhaps the most impressive one ever held in our nation's capital. All of the important figures of the day were there, including the country's President at the time, Zachary Taylor. She was buried in Washington, but nine years later her remains were moved back to Virginia to rest beside James at "Montpelier."

Elizabeth Kortright Monroe

Born: June 30, 1768
Died: September 23, 1830
First Lady: 1817-1825

This dark-haired, blue-eyed beauty was born in New York City to Hannah and Lawrence Kortright. Her father, a founder of the New York Chamber of Commerce, was a wealthy merchant, and so Elizabeth enjoyed the trappings of growing up as a member of New York's upper crust. Fluent in French, she traveled throughout Europe, and attended many social functions. It was at such a function that she met James Monroe, who was, at the time, a delegate to the Continental Congress. In February 1786, the 17-year-old Elizabeth and the 27-year-old James were married — in spite of her parents' reservations (they apparently felt that James came from a family that was of a much lower social circle).

The Monroes had their first child, a daughter, only ten months into their marriage. Two more children, a son and another daughter, would follow, but their son would pass away before his third birthday. They settled down in Charlottesville, Virginia, near Monroe's good friend, Thomas Jefferson.

In 1790, James was elected to the United States Senate, and so the family moved to

Philadelphia, which was the federal capital at that time. Four years later, President Washington asked Monroe to be our country's Minister to France. James gladly accepted, and so, in the summer of 1794, the family was once again on the move, this time to the magical city of Paris, France.

One of the highlights of Elizabeth's life took place while she was living in France: with the French Revolution raging about her, she successfully engineered the release of Madame Lafayette, the wife of American revolutionary hero Marquis de Lafayette, from prison, where she had been awaiting her execution. Because of this heroic act, the French aristocracy took to calling Elizabeth, "*la belle Americaine.*"

Things had not gone as well for her husband, however, and in 1797, dissatisfied with his performance, American officials recalled Monroe, and the couple returned home in the spring. They would return to France, however, in 1803 when President Jefferson requested that James help negotiate what would later be known as the Louisiana Purchase. Once again, Elizabeth ingratiated herself to the French with her charm and grace.

Ideally, Elizabeth's upbringing and European experience should have prepared her for life as the First Lady. Unfortunately, Elizabeth had to follow in the footsteps of the unbelievably popular Dolley Madison. And when, upon becoming the First Lady in 1817, Elizabeth put an end to Dolley's practice of either calling on or returning the calls of the ladies who counted themselves among the upper crust of Washington society, she received a great deal of negative publicity. A private person who was also suffering from rheumatism, Elizabeth did not feel she could keep up the hectic schedule that had been set by her predecessor. Unfortunately, neither high society nor the public at large were sympathetic to her desires.

Her relationship with the women of Washington worsened when Elizabeth and her eldest daughter Eliza (who was by now handling many of her ill mother's duties) refused to throw an elaborate wedding for the youngest daughter in the family, Maria. A small, private affair was held, much to the displeasure of the public.

The Monroe's second term in office saw quite a bit of thawing in their relationship with Washington society. Their affairs were by now well attended, and Elizabeth's ill health and desire for privacy was better understood by all. The couple retired to Oak Hill, their home in Virginia, in 1825. Three years later, Elizabeth died at the age of 62, finally succumbing to the rheumatism that had plagued her for a good portion of her life.

Louisa Catherine Johnson Adams
Born: February 12, 1775
Died: May 14, 1852
First Lady: 1825-1829

Louisa Adams was the only First Lady to be born in a foreign country. Her father was Joshua Johnson, the London representative of an American tobacco company. Joshua was the brother of Thomas Johnson, the Governor of Maryland and one of the men who signed the Declaration of Independence. Elizabeth's mother was Catherine Nuth, an Englishwoman.

When the American Revolution broke out, Joshua Johnson moved his family to Nantes, France, which would be where Louisa would spend the majority of her childhood. As a result, Louisa was fluent in both French and English (not to mention Greek). Her education was extremely solid; in fact, it is often said that Louisa was the most well-educated woman to ever inhabit the White House.

Louisa first met John Quincy in England in 1795. While the two of them did not have a passionate courtship, they were nevertheless married in July 1797. John Quincy's family did not at first approve of the marriage, primarily because they did not trust Louisa's father. Their hunch proved to be correct when, only two weeks after the marriage, Joshua Johnson announced that he was bankrupt.

The American press was not thrilled with the union either. John Quincy's father was newly ensconced in the White House, and the newspapers loudly complained that the President's son had married a foreigner. It did not matter to them that she was actually half-American. Despite the fact that their marriage got off to a rocky start, the Adams' would have a productive and happy relationship. Louisa gave birth to four children, three of whom lived to adulthood.

Immediately after their wedding, the couple moved to Berlin, where John Quincy was the American minister to Prussia. In 1801, they returned to the United States, and John Quincy ran for and won a Senate seat representing his home state of Massachusetts. Louisa was happy to be in the United States, because it allowed her to be reunited with her family, who were now living in America as a result of her father's new position as Director of Stamps in Washington D.C.

After John Quincy resigned from the Senate in 1808, he was offered the position of Minister to Russia. Accepting the post, he insisted that Louisa leave their two eldest children in America and take only the baby. Life in Russia proved to be extremely hard on Louisa. The weather was freezing cold and she often suffered from migraine headaches. She missed her two sons and felt lost and lonely.

In 1815, Louisa set off on the most harrowing adventure of her life. John Quincy was in Paris, helping to negotiate the peace treaty which would end the War of 1812. He wrote to Louisa, telling her to come join him. In spite of the fact that two thousand miles of frozen terrain separated the couple, Louisa and her son, Charles Francis, boarded a coach with three servants and set off for Paris.

After weeks of deep snow and frozen rivers, their money stolen and the servants having long since deserted them, the mother and child neared Paris. Suddenly, however, they began to encounter angry French troops. Napoleon had escaped from Elba and was headed back to Paris, and the French soldiers, spotting the Russian markings on Louisa's coach, assumed she was Russian herself. It was only when Louisa began shouting "*Vive Napoleon*," and explained in French that she was actually American that the troops allowed her to proceed unharmed. When she and her son finally arrived at John Quincy's hotel, she found her husband upset with her because she had arrived so late. Needless to say, John Quincy was not an easy man to have for a husband.

From Paris the couple traveled to London, where John Quincy served as Minister to

England. It was here that Louisa was reunited with her two sons, George Washington and John, after a seven year separation.

In 1817, John Quincy was appointed Secretary of State by President Monroe. It was a position he would hold for the next eight years. The highlight for Louisa during this period was the party she put together in 1824 for General Andrew Jackson on the 10th anniversary of the Battle of New Orleans. The event was attended by nearly 1,000 people, and was the talk of the town for months on end.

The years Louisa spent as First Lady were not particularly happy ones. She was often ill with her migraine headaches, and her husband was not a popular President. Once, writing a letter to her husband, she claimed that she felt like a "bird in a cage."

Three years after John Quincy had lost his bid for reelection, the couple returned to Washington when the former President won election as the Representative from Massachusetts. Louisa and John Quincy would remain in Washington until their deaths. He died 17 years later while working at his desk in the House of Representatives, and she passed away four years after his death, on May 14, 1852, at the age of 77.

Rachel Donelson Jackson

Born: June 15, 1767
Died: December 22, 1828
First Lady: Died before husband took office

Rachel Jackson's life story is among the most tragic of all the first ladies. A child of the frontier, she was born in Virginia, and traveled some 2,000 miles with her family into the Tennessee wilderness when she was only 12 years old. Her teenage years were spent sewing, cooking, and helping out around the colony; there was very little time for schooling, although she did manage to learn how to read and write.

When she was 17, her family moved to Kentucky. By now, Rachel was extremely attractive, with beautiful brown eyes and long, dark hair. It was in Kentucky that she met, and soon married, Lewis Robards. Robards, however, turned out to be an insanely jealous man. After four years of marriage, Rachel couldn't take Robards' accusations any longer, and she moved back to Tennessee, where her mother now ran a Nashville boarding house.

Andrew Jackson, a young lawyer practicing in Nashville, met and fell in love with Rachel. Robards objected to their relationship, and on more than one occasion he and Jackson almost settled the matter with guns. Eventually, however, Jackson received news that Robards had given up and had been granted a divorce from Rachel. Andrew and Rachel were immediately married.

Trouble came two years later when it was revealed that Robards had never been granted a divorce. Now, Rachel and Andrew were being accused of adultery. Robards sued for divorce on the grounds of adultery and won easily. Andrew and Rachel were soon married once again — this time legally — but the damage had been done: the accusations of adultery would haunt the couple for the rest of their lives.

Throughout Jackson's career, no matter how much he tried to explain his side of the story, his political opponents would attack him for his relationship with Rachel. To make matters worse, Rachel was often ridiculed for her frontier upbringing and unfamiliar ways in high society.

By the time Jackson was running for the presidency in 1828, the attack from his political opponents had reached new heights in bad taste. One newspaper asked if "a convicted adulteress and her paramour husband" should be placed in the White House. Rachel was growing increasingly ashamed. By now a religious convert, she felt a tremendous amount of guilt. The thought of being the First Lady horrified her. While being fitted for an outfit she would wear to her husband's inauguration, she overheard some women in the shop making derogatory comments about her and she had a heart attack. She passed away five days later. Her funeral was the most elaborate one Nashville had ever seen.

Hannah Hoes Van Buren

Born: February 4, 1776
Died: February 5, 1819
First Lady: Died before husband took office

Hannah Van Buren was born in the same Dutch community as her future husband, Martin. They were actually distant cousins — his mother was related to the Hoes family. The two children were educated at the same small school, allegedly by the teacher who Washington Irving would later make famous as Ichabod Crane in his classic tale, "The Legend of Sleepy Hollow."

When the couple turned 18, they agreed to get married — some day. In the meantime, however, Martin concentrated on his career as a lawyer and later as a surrogate judge. Finally, in 1807, some 13 years after he had promised to marry her, Martin impulsively put together a wedding, and the couple was joined in matrimony.

Hannah gave birth to three sons in the early years of their marriage. For the most part, Hannah raised her boys without the help of Martin, who was often living in another city, pursuing his career in politics. When he became the Attorney General of New York State in 1815, he moved the family from their home on the Hudson to the state capital of Albany. In 1817, Hannah gave birth to another son, but it was a difficult pregnancy and Hannah became very ill. She subsequently developed tuberculosis and passed away on February 5, 1819.

After her death, Martin gave the children to relatives and friends and resumed his active career. He was elected President in 1836. He died in 1862, lonely, sick, and forgotten by many.

Anna Tuthill Symmes Harrison
Born: July 25, 1775
Died: February 25, 1864
First Lady: 1841

Anna's mother died exactly one year after her birth, and when she was four years old, her father decided to bring her to Long Island to live with her grandparents. It was 1778, and the family's home in Morristown, New Jersey was being threatened by British troops. Her father, Colonel John Cleves Symmes, felt that she would be safer on Long Island.

Donning a dead British officer's uniform and placing Anna on the front of his saddle, Colonel Symmes rode across the British lines on a perilous journey, disguised as a British officer. A few days later they arrived, safe and sound, at Anna's grandparents' house. Colonel Symmes returned to the fighting and Anna would not see her father for five long years.

Anna was well educated at the Clinton Academy on Long Island and Miss Graham's Boarding School in New York City. She loved to read and play the piano. She was a petite woman, quiet and serious with brown eyes and brown hair.

In 1794, Symmes bought a great deal of land in Ohio. The following year, he moved there with Anna and his third wife. At the time, Ohio was the land of pioneers, wild and untamed, and quite a bit different than the cosmopolitan atmosphere of New York to which Anna had grown accustomed.

Anna made the best of things, however, and in 1795, while visiting her sister in Kentucky, she met William Henry Harrison, a lieutenant in the army. They fell in love, but Anna's father did not think that Harrison had much of a future outside of the army, and he refused to allow the couple to get married. On November 25, 1795, against her father's wishes, Anna married Harrison while Judge Symmes was away on a business trip. When Anna's father returned he was incensed; it would be years before he would accept William Henry Harrison as his son-in-law.

The couple settled in North Bend, Ohio, and over the years Anna gave birth to 10 children. When Harrison was elected as the territorial Governor of Indiana, the family moved to Vincennes, Indiana, to a house they named "Grouseland." During this period, Anna did a great deal of entertaining, including hosting visiting Indian chiefs.

The family returned to North Bend in 1811, and for the next few years Harrison was away attending to his military duties as a major-general in the Kentucky militia during the War of 1812. Throughout this period, Anna concentrated on raising the children and running the household. She hired a tutor for her children so that they could be educated at home.

Unfortunately, Anna would suffer a great deal of tragedy in the years to come, including the deaths of six children by the time her husband was elected President in 1840. She would go on to survive all of her children but one, John Scott, who would subsequently father Benjamin Harrison, the 23rd President of the United States.

Anna was 65 when she became First Lady, and wasn't well enough to attend the inauguration, much less face up to the new duties which were about to be thrust upon her. In fact, when she heard the news of her husband's victory, she is reported to have said, "I wish that my husband's friends had left him where he is, happy and contented in retirement."

William Henry Harrison, however, died only one month after taking office — the result of his giving the longest inaugural speech ever while a freezing cold rain descended upon the crowd. He had stubbornly refused to wear a coat or a hat and caught pneumonia. One has to wonder if things would have turned out differently if Anna had been there to choose her husband's outfit on the day of his inauguration. Anna's stint as First Lady became the shortest on record. She had been packing to leave for the capital when she heard the news of her husband's death. She would remain in Ohio until her death at the age of 89.

It is interesting to note that Anna was the only First Lady who lived through the four most important American wars of the 18th and 19th centuries: the Revolution, the War of 1812, the Mexican War, and the Civil War. Additionally, while Anna was married to one President and was the grandmother of another, she never visited Washington D.C.

Letitia Christian Tyler

Born: November 12, 1790
Died: September 10, 1842
First Lady: 1841-1842

Letitia was born at "Cedar Grove," her family's estate in Virginia. She grew up surrounded by a large family, as well as a host of servants and slaves. She spent her entire childhood on the plantation, and was even educated in her home.

A petite girl with deep, dark eyes and smooth, olive skin, Letitia met John Tyler when they were both still teenagers (he was 18 and she was a year younger). For some unknown reason, Letitia's parents had reservations about any marriage plans for their daughter — it apparently didn't matter that Tyler had become an attorney when he was 20 years old, or that he was elected to the Virginia House of Delegates only a year later. It wasn't until 1812, when John's father died, leaving him a fair amount of land and money, that Mr. Christian consented to the wedding. Five long years had passed since Letitia and John had originally met. It has been said that John did not even kiss his fiancee's hand until three weeks before they were married.

While John pursued his political career, Letitia oversaw the work that was going on at their busy plantation. In fact, Letitia was so competent at her job that Tyler never had to worry about financial matters, thus lifting a great burden that allowed him to concentrate solely upon his political career. Along with running the plantation, Letitia loved to knit and tend to the lovely roses in her garden. She also, of course, found time to raise her seven children, although one of them died in infancy.

Letitia did not care for Washington, choosing instead to stay in her beloved Virginia while her husband served as a Senator. Likewise, Letitia never really got to enjoy the fruits of being a First Lady. She suffered a stroke in 1839, and was still ill and confined to a wheelchair by the time John took over the presidency in 1841. Her only public appearance occurred at her daughter's wedding in January, 1842. In September of that same year, Letitia had another stroke and died at the age of 51.

Julia Gardiner Tyler

Born: May 4, 1820
Died: July 10, 1889
First Lady: 1844-1845

Julia was born into a well-to-do family. Her father, David Gardiner, was a New York state senator for a brief time, but it was from her mother, Juliana McLachlan, that the Gardiner's had acquired a great deal of wealth and land (Juliana had inherited all of this from her father). Julia was educated at the exclusive Madame N.D. Chagray institute in Manhattan. When she was 19, she somewhat naively appeared in an advertisement for Bogert and McCamly, a New York City department store. The ad labeled her as the "Rose of Long Island." To compound the embarrassment to the family, the front page of the *Brooklyn Daily News* printed a love poem written by a young man who had fallen for Julia after seeing her in the advertisement.

To escape the awkward situation, the Gardiners took an extended vacation to Europe, and eventually landed in Washington D.C. It was here, in January of 1842, that Julia met President John Tyler. Julia was by now a beautiful young lady, with long dark hair and a gorgeous complexion. Tyler was still married however, so it wasn't until the next year, after his wife had died, that John began to think about Julia in romantic terms.

The much younger Julia — she was 30 years the President's junior — initially rebuffed Tyler's advances. She turned down his proposal of marriage in February of 1843, but continued to correspond with him when her family moved away from Washington in March. One year later, with Tyler's long distance wooing having continued unabated, the Gardiner's returned to Washington. The family was sailing aboard a new propeller-driven warship, the *Princeton*, with the President and hundreds of other special guests, when tragedy occurred. The ship's main gun misfired, and the resulting explosion killed eight people, including Julia's father.

A distraught Julia was comforted by the President and, perhaps now seeking a figure to replace the father she had so tragically lost, Julia finally agreed to marry John. The wedding took place four months after the death of Julia's father, on June 26, 1844. Tyler's daughters from his previous marriage, echoing the reaction of many people across the country, were outraged by the wedding. They felt it had occurred too soon after their own mother's death, and the fact that Tyler was 54 years old and Julia was 24 years old certainly didn't make matters any easier.

Julia made the most of her reign as First Lady. She created a royal image for herself by hiring a press agent and surrounding herself with what can only be called a "court" — maids of honor who attended to her every need. With her own family's money she refurbished the White House, restoring what had become a somewhat rundown building into a gleaming palace. When it came time for her and John to leave the White House — only eight months after she had become First Lady — she threw the most lavish party Washington had ever seen. Thousands attended the ball, and they literally devoured the seemingly endless parade of food, champagne and wine that was being served.

From Washington, Julia moved with John to "Sherwood Forest" in Virginia. They started a family here, and she eventually gave birth to five sons and two daughters (the last child was born when John was over 70 years old!). The division between the North and the South was beginning to deepen, and the Tylers found their allegiance leaning towards the Southern states. John was soon elected to the Confederate House of Representatives. In January of 1862, just before he was going to begin his term in the Congress, Julia dreamed that John was dying and she rushed to Richmond to be by his side. It turned out to be a false alarm — when Julia arrived, she found John to be in perfect health, fully recovered from his illness. Four days later, however, Tyler entered her room, his hands grasping his throat just as she had envisioned in her dream. He dropped dead; the cause was never known. He was 71 years old.

The years following her husband's death were extremely difficult ones for Julia. Sherwood Forest was burned by Union troops, her mother died, and she became involved in several lawsuits against her own brother over the terms of her mother's will. She managed to survive however, and by the mid-1870s her life was back on track, both financially and personally. She returned to her flamboyant ways, and lived out the remainder of her life in style. She died at the age of 69 on July 10, 1889 in the Richmond Hotel, across the hall from where her husband had died more than 25 years earlier.

Sarah Childress Polk

Born: September 4, 1803
Died: August 14, 1891
First Lady: 1845-1849

Sarah Childress Polk was born into a well-to-do Tennessee family. Her father, Captain Joel Childress, was a wealthy planter, and her mother, Elizabeth Whitsitt, was a member of one of the families who originally settled in Tennessee. After attending private school in Nashville, Sarah, at the age of 15, was sent to the prestigious Moravian Female Academy in Salem, North Carolina. She received a formidable education at the school, with a heavy emphasis on religion.

It is believed that Sarah first met James Polk in Murfreesboro when she was 12 and he was 19. Polk was evidently quite taken with the tall, exotic-looking young girl, for he waited patiently until she turned 16 before he began seriously courting her. They were married four years later, in what can only be described as a joyous celebration that lasted two weeks. The pair would not have any children.

Polk was by now a member of the Tennessee State Legislature, and the following year he won election to Congress, and the couple moved to Washington. A deeply religious pair, Sarah and James kept their noses to the grindstone and saw their hard work pay off in spades. By 1835, James was chosen to be the Speaker of the House of Representatives, and in 1839 he returned to Tennessee, where he took over the governership of the state. James was elected President in 1845, and the couple returned to Washington.

The Polk's years in the White House were

marked by new rules which adhered to the strict Presbyterian code that Sarah and her husband followed. Dancing, drinking, and card playing were forbidden at all affairs. Remarkably, Sarah was still considered to be a popular First Lady. She was a wonderful conversationalist, and dressed with great style in tasteful silks, velvets and satins. She established the tradition of having a Thanksgiving dinner at the White House, and worked her tail off as her husband's personal secretary. During Polk's four years in office, the couple did not take a single vacation and normally worked 14-hour days.

By the time Polk left office, he was thin and frail, probably the result of working too hard. He died only three months after leaving the White House, on June 15, 1849. Sarah would live for another 42 years. She remained at her home in Nashville, known as "Polk Place," never leaving except to go to church. During the Civil War, her home was unofficially declared to be neutral ground, and she entertained both Confederate and Union generals. In a tribute to her husband's memory, she wore at least one article of black clothing every day for the rest of her life. When she passed away in 1891, she was buried in the same tomb as her beloved James.

Margaret Mackall Smith Taylor

Born: September 21, 1788
Died: August 18, 1852
First Lady: 1849-1850

Not much is known about Margaret Taylor's childhood. She was born in Calvert County, Maryland in 1788 to Walter Smith and Ann Mackall. Her father had fought in the Revolutionary War, and her mother died when Margaret was a teenager. When she was 21, she met a 24-year-old lieutenant, Zachary Taylor, while visiting her sister in Kentucky. They were married a year later at the home of her sister.

The couple was living in Jefferson County, Kentucky, when Zachary was promoted to captain and assigned to Fort Knox. For the next three decades, Margaret would essentially be rootless, constantly shuttling back and forth between Kentucky and Fort Knox. This lifestyle also kept her separated from her six children for much of the time, as they remained in Kentucky whenever she would visit her husband in Fort Knox.

Taylor continued his rise in the army, and in 1819, when he was promoted to lieutenant colonel, he was also reassigned to Louisiana. The whole family moved to the bayou country, but what followed was heartbreak and sadness. During a horrific four month period, the couple lost two of their youngest daughters to malaria, and Margaret herself became quite ill. When she recovered some of her strength, she insisted that the remaining children be sent away to school. This left her extremely lonely, but at least she knew her children would remain healthy.

Tragedy struck again in 1835, however, when the Taylor's daughter, Knox, died of malaria. Knox had married Jefferson Davis, the man who would one day be the President of the Confederacy, and, in spite of her parent's warnings, moved to Louisiana. A month after they arrived she caught malaria and died. It would be years before Margaret's father, who had never approved of the marriage, forgave Davis.

The Taylors finally got the chance to settle down in 1841, when Zachary was given a permanent post at Baton Rouge. The pipe-smoking Margaret was by now 53 years old, and had never known a place as an adult that she could seriously call home. For the past three decades, she had moved from fort to fort with her husband, and endured many lonely nights while he was off fighting in one battle or another.

But her happiness would be short-lived once again, for in 1845 General Taylor was called away to Texas to fight in the Mexican War. Taylor returned from the war a hero and was soon elected President. Margaret was extremely saddened and angered by this turn of events. She had been apart from her husband for too many years, and feared that Taylor's election would mean even more of the same. She refused to attend any functions in Washington, turning over all hostessing duties to her daughter, Mary Elizabeth Bliss. Instead, Margaret remained in seclusion in her second floor apartment inside the White House — a room that was decorated exactly like her home in Baton Rouge.

Taylor died suddenly in the second year of his term. A distraught Margaret went to live with her son in Mississippi, where she taught Sunday school until her death two years later. Thus, the Taylors became the first presidential couple to both die before the husband's four-year term was officially completed.

Abigail Powers Fillmore

Born: March 13, 1798
Died: March 30, 1853
First Lady: 1850-1853

Abigail's father, Reverend Lemuel Powers, died when she was only two, leaving her mother, Abigail Newland, alone to care for her and her older brother. The family moved from their home in Saratoga County, New York, to a more isolated part of the state, where there was greater opportunity and where the cost of living was low.

It was in this remote western part of New York that Abigail first met Millard Fillmore. Surprisingly, in spite of the fact that they were raised only a few miles from each other, the couple would not meet until she was 21 and he was 19. Even more unusual was the manner in which they met: Abigail was teaching school and Millard, desperate for a proper education, had enrolled in her class. At only two years younger than his teacher, he was by far her oldest student.

It took many years for their romance to bloom. Millard eventually moved to a town near Buffalo where he studied law. Eventually, however, he returned to his hometown and married Abigail at the home of her brother. Their wedding took place on February 5, 1826, some seven years after they had first met.

The couple moved to Aurora, New York, where Millard set up a law practice. An early feminist model, Abigail continued to work as a teacher despite the fact that she was now married. They had two children over the next few years, and Millard began his political career during this happy period.

As Millard continued his rise in politics, the family's financial picture became rosier and rosier. They moved into a beautiful home in Buffalo, and eventually settled in Albany in 1848 when Millard was elected as Comptroller of the state of New York. During this time, Abigail continued to indulge in her passion for reading books, and her and her husband's library soon grew to include more than four thousand volumes.

When Fillmore took over the presidency, Abigail did not immediately join him as she was ill. Several months into his term, she recovered and was finally able to take her rightful place as the nation's First Lady. During her tenure as First Lady, Abigail established the first presidential library in the White House, installed the first bath tub in the White House, and ordered that all cooking be done on an iron stove as opposed to the fireplace. Writers, artists and musicians were often invited to the White House to speak or perform, including Washington Irving. Indeed, Abigail brought a great deal of culture to the executive mansion.

While attending the inauguration of Franklin Pierce, Abigail caught a cold from standing in the rain that was pouring down during the ceremony. Her cold turned into pneumonia, and she died less than a month after her husband left office. She was buried in Buffalo, New York.

Jane Means Appleton Pierce

Born: March 12, 1806
Died: December 2, 1863
First Lady: 1853-1857

When Jane Pierce was a baby, her father, Reverend Jesse Appleton, was appointed the President of Maine's Bowdoin college. Because of her father's position, Jane and her five brothers and sisters received an excellent education. Jane's mother, Elizabeth Means, came from an extremely wealthy family, and so Jane certainly did not lack for very much as a child. Her health, however, was frail, partly a result of her father's belief that fresh air and physical exertion were not beneficial for girls.

The circumstances of how the slender, shy Jane met Franklin Pierce remain unknown, although it is thought that they were introduced while Franklin was a student at Bowdoin. After a long, six-year engagement, they were married on November 19, 1834.

At the time of their marriage, Pierce's career was in full swing. He had a successful law practice and represented New Hampshire in Congress. They moved to Washington for a while, then returned to New Hampshire when the congressional session ended. In 1836, Jane gave birth to a baby boy, but unfortunately the infant died three days later. It was an exceedingly difficult period for both Franklin and Jane.

In spite of the fact that Franklin was elected to the Senate later that year, troubles continued to pound away at Jane. Many members of her family passed away during the year, and her health was not good. She disliked Washington, preferring to stay in her native New Hampshire. Happiness arrived in August of the following year when she gave birth to a healthy boy, whom they named Frank Robert. Another son, Benjamin, came along two years later.

At Jane's urging, Franklin retired from politics in 1842 and the Pierce family moved to Concord. Tragedy, however, soon struck again when four-year-old Frank Robert died of typhoid fever.

With the exception of Franklin's short stint as a brigadier-general in the Mexican War, the Pierce's lived a quiet life for ten years in Concord. But when the Democratic convention selected Franklin as their candidate for President in 1852, their peaceful life underwent an enormous change. Jane had fainted when she heard the news of the nomination, and her prayers that her husband lose the election were not answered, as Pierce stormed to victory.

Two months later, tragedy struck yet again. While traveling by train, the family was involved in a terrible accident that left their only son, 11-year-old Benny, dead. The child was the only person killed during the train wreck, and he died in front of his parents' eyes. Jane was so distraught that she could not accompany her husband to Washington in March for his inauguration. Likewise, when she finally did come to Washington, she was unable to perform any of her duties as First Lady. Instead, she spent her time hidden away in her room, writing letters to her deceased son.

Finally, on January 1, 1855, some two years after her son's death, Jane made her first appearance as First Lady. While she did not look well, it was enough to get her going again, and during the remaining two years of her husband's term, she made more and more public appearances at his side.

After Pierce's term ended, he retired from politics and took his wife on an extended vacation through Europe. Jane, however, was rarely in good spirits, and on December 2, 1863, she died of tuberculosis. She is buried in Concord, New Hampshire.

Mary Todd Lincoln

Born: December 13, 1818
Died: July 16, 1882
First Lady: 1861-1865

Mary Lincoln was raised in a wealthy Kentucky household (her father was a banker) where there were always plenty of slaves around to attend to the family's every need. While the slaves were treated benevolently, Mary was raised with the belief that there was nothing wrong with slavery. She was well-educated at an upper crust boarding school.

When she was 19, Mary moved to Springfield, Illinois, to join her sister, who had relocated there several years earlier. While attending a cotillion, she was introduced to Abraham Lincoln. A volatile courtship followed, and despite the fact that the couple was not necessarily well-matched — Mary was known for her acid tongue and her violent temper while Abe was quiet and melancholy — they were engaged, with a wedding set for early 1841. When the big day came, however, Lincoln, suffering from depression, left his bride standing alone at the altar. A second engagement led to a wedding in Mary's sister's home on November 4, 1842.

Lincoln's career moved along slowly. He

was a fairly inconsequential Congressman for a term, and his law career was no great shakes either. In the meantime, Mary gave birth to four sons, although one passed away at the age of four.

Abe continued to work hard, and his law career finally began to take off. He made an unsuccessful run for the vice presidency in 1856, but the great speeches he gave were beginning to earn him fame and accolades. In 1860, Abe campaigned for President and ran away with the election. Mary couldn't have been happier; she took off for New York and bought a tremendous amount of clothing and accessories.

Mary was not a popular First Lady. She continued spending money as if it were going out of style, despite the fact that the Civil War was heating up and everyone in Washington was trying to cut back on their expenses. While she saw herself as worldly and sophisticated — she was, in fact, well-read and extremely witty — others saw her as a woman who grew up as a big fish in a small town; they considered Springfield to be nothing but a backwater village. The fact that she had moved from Kentucky to Springfield years earlier branded her as a defector to the many Southerners who lived in Washington. Likewise, the Northerners accused her of being a Southern sympathizer, especially after she invited her sister — whose husband had died while fighting for the South — to live in the White House. It should also be noted that Mary's visits to local hospitals to bring food and clothing to the wounded soldiers, as well as the fact that she often wrote letters to the soldiers' families, were acts of kindness the general public knew nothing about.

When the Lincoln's son, Willie, died on February 20, 1862, Mary went into a tailspin from which she would never recover. Her migraine headaches worsened, she suffered from bizarre mood swings, became insanely jealous of any women who got anywhere near her husband, and continued to pile up debts from her shopping sprees (she now owed nearly $30,000 to a variety of merchants). It has been reported that she once bought 3,000 pairs of gloves.

After her husband's assassination in April 1865, Mary retreated behind closed doors for more than a month. When she finally emerged, she took her two sons and fled to Chicago. Tragedy struck again when pneumonia took her son in July 1871. She now had only one son left, but because her behavior — which included hallucinations — had become so erratic, her daughter-in-law refused to allow Mary to visit their home.

Essentially homeless, Mary was forced to move from hotel room to hotel room. She imagined that she was flat out broke when the contrary was the case — she once had over $50,000 in cash tucked into her corset — and often thought that there were people who were trying to kill her. Finally, in May 1875, Mary's son, Robert, had her declared legally insane and she was committed to a hospital. The night before she left she tried to commit suicide, but failed because a wise druggist had substituted sugar for the laudanum she had requested. After much legal wrangling, she was released several months later, and after a brief stay with her sister, she took off for Europe, where for four years she traveled from country to country and from town to town, often staying in run down hotels. She eventually returned to the United States on the ship *l'Amerique*. Actress Sarah Bernhardt, a fellow passenger, saved Mary from taking a terrible fall on the deck of the ship. When *l'Amerique* docked in New York, there were thousands of people there to greet Bernhardt, but all of them ignored the presence of Mary. Two years after she had returned to the United States, Mary suffered a stroke and died at the home of her sister at the age of 63.

Eliza McCardle Johnson

Born: October 4, 1810
Died: January 15, 1876
First Lady: 1865-1869

Eliza Johnson was born and raised in a poor town in the mountains of eastern Tennessee. Her father, an innkeeper and shoemaker, died when she was a small child, leaving Eliza and her mother penniless. The pair somehow managed to survive, and Eliza was even able to obtain a basic education.

One day, when Eliza was 16, a family arrived in her hometown. They had come down from the Great Smoky Mountains, and had brought a cart filled with all of their belongings. In front of the cart strode a well-built, 18-year-old man named Andrew Johnson. The young man asked Eliza if she knew if there were any cabins for rent in the area. Eliza sent the family to a local shopkeeper. It was truly love at first sight.

Andrew established himself as a tailor and began to court Eliza. On May 5, 1827, the 19-year-old Andrew married his 17-year-old love. Ironically, they were married by a distant relative of Abraham Lincoln. They moved into a two room house, and converted the front room into a shop where Andrew could ply his trade.

Despite his lack of education, Andrew displayed a great deal of confidence and strength. Eliza recognized his capacity for greatness and pushed him to better educate himself.

Beginning with his election as the town Alderman in 1831, Johnson quickly moved through a succession of important positions, from town Mayor (1832), to member of the Tennessee legislature (1835), to Congressman (1842), to Governor of Tennessee (1853), to Senator (1857). During this period, Eliza watched over the family finances and gave birth to five children. The birth of her last child in 1854 was a difficult one, however, and left Eliza weak and ill.

With the outbreak of the Civil War, the Johnson household was thrown into a dangerous situation. Johnson was a vocal opponent of secession, and his Southern neighbors were out for blood. With a stubborn resolve, Andrew insisted that his family remain at their home in Tennessee, even while war raged around them. They were not able to stay long however, and Eliza had to flee to a nearby county when the Johnson home was taken over by Southern troops. Johnson was now in Nashville, serving as Lincoln's personally appointed Military Governor of Tennessee, and could not get through enemy lines to save his wife. Months passed. Finally, in September of 1862, Eliza was granted permission to take her family through the Confederate lines and join her husband. It was, to say the least, a harrowing journey, but Eliza and her children made it safely, arriving in Nashville a little over a month later.

With the assassination of Lincoln, Eliza was suddenly thrust into the role of First Lady. Even though her husband had been Vice President, she had been living a relatively quiet life in Tennessee when her husband was forced to take over the presidency.

Eliza was not in very good health during her time in Washington, and thus did not participate in many of the events normally attended by first ladies. She only appeared at two public functions, one of which was a party thrown in honor of her husband's 60th birthday. For the most part she remained in her room, knitting and reading the Bible. Eliza did manage, however, to restore the White House — which had been virtually destroyed by both looters in the aftermath of Lincoln's death and by a lack of funds during the Civil War — to its former glory.

In the wake of Johnson's difficult presidency, the couple moved back to Tennessee. An extremely ill and sickly Eliza would somehow manage to live for seven more years, dying at the age of 65, a mere six months after her husband's death. They are both buried in Greenville, Tennessee.

Julia Dent Grant

Born: January 26, 1826
Died: December 14, 1902
First Lady: 1869-1877

Julia Grant was born and raised on her father's enormous farm just outside of St. Louis. She was sent away at the age of 10 to a private school, where she received a well-rounded education. Julia met her future husband, Lieutenant Ulysses S. Grant, when Grant was visiting her home in 1844. Grant was a friend of Julia's brother, having met him at West Point.

A few months later, after helping her cross over the swollen Mississippi River, Grant proposed to Julia, who readily agreed, but her father did not approve of her marrying a simple soldier. Thus began a long engagement that was made even longer when Grant was ordered to ride with Zachary Taylor's army in Mexico. The Mexican War would end up separating Julia and Ulysses until the summer of 1848, but upon his return they were immediately married. While Julia's parents had finally relented and welcomed Ulysses into the family, his parents refused to attend the wedding because they did not support slavery and were angered by the Dent's ownership of a large number of slaves. Ironically, the best man and two of the ushers would eventually serve in the Confederate Army.

The next several years would see the Grants living in naval stations on Lake Ontario and in Detroit. Julia had two children during this period, and had to contend with harsh winters and her husband's drinking problem, a weakness that would soon provide a series of enormous tests. In 1852, Grant was sent to the Pacific Coast. Unable to bear being separated from his wife and children, he began to drink heavily, and was eventually forced to resign from the army.

Grant returned to St. Louis and he and Julia settled on a farm which Julia's father had given them. The next few years at "Hardscrabble," as their home was known, were extremely difficult. Money was tight and Grant proved to be a failure as a farmer. Two more children were born during this period.

In 1860, the family moved to Galena, Illinois, where Grant went to work at his family's leather store. By this time, he was widely regarded as being a complete failure, but the fighting at Fort Sumter would soon change both his and Julia's lives forever.

Throughout the Civil War, Julia and her sons traveled with Grant. Their 13-year-old son, Fred, even fought alongside Ulysses, and during one battle he sustained a slight wound to his leg. For her part, Julia would often tend to the injured, sew their torn uniforms, and lift their spirits. In what is known as the *River Queen* incident, Mary Lincoln publicly reprimanded Julia for sitting next to her on a couch without first asking for Mary's permission. Infuriated, Julia swore to never again socialize with the Lincolns. Three weeks later, the Grants declined the Lincolns' invitation to go to the theater — a decision they regretted for the rest of their lives. Who knows if the great Ulysses would have been able to save the President on that fateful night?

Ulysses' military genius culminated with the surrender of General Robert E. Lee at Appomattox on April 9, 1865. Julia was now married to the greatest hero in the country; her patience had finally paid off and those terribly dark days of the previous decades were now far behind them.

Grant was elected President in 1868. While Julia's debut at the Inaugural Ball was something of a disaster — the party was full of disorder and chaos — her subsequent receptions were extremely successful. She hosted parties for emperors and Kings, and generally stayed above the criticism that surrounded her husband's administration.

At the end of Grant's second term, the couple took a trip around the world where they were greeted as heroes in major cities throughout Europe, Asia and Africa. Two years later they arrived home nearly penniless, but managed to purchase a home in New York City with the help of friends and business associates.

The Grants made several poor investments, however, and by 1885 they found themselves bankrupt. Mark Twain came to the rescue with an offer to publish Ulysses' autobiography. Despite suffering from throat cancer, Grant managed to finish his memoirs in July of 1885, just one week before he died.

Julia would survive her beloved husband by 17 years. She remained close to her children and her grandchildren, and even struck up a friendship with the widow of Jefferson Davis in her final years. When she died on December 14, 1902, Julia was buried next to Ulysses in what is now known as Grant's Tomb, on Riverside Drive in New York City.

Lucy Ware Webb Hayes

Born: August 28, 1831
Died: June 25, 1889
First Lady: 1877-1881

Lucy Webb was born into a family who could trace their family roots back to the Revolutionary War, where they had fought for our country's freedom. In recompense for their bravery, the members of the Webb family received some land in Ohio. By the time Lucy arrived into the world, her family owned large parcels of property and many slaves. Her father, James Webb, was anti-slavery, however, and in 1833 he went to Kentucky in order to sign the papers which would not only free his slaves, but arrange for them to go back to Liberia. During this trip, however, he became ill with cholera and died; Lucy was two years old at the time.

Lucy grew up with this anti-slavery attitude, and was also imbued with a strong sense of religion. She met Rutherford Hayes in Delaware, Ohio, when she was a teenager after the couple's respective mothers thought that they would be a good match. Lucy had moved there with her mother so that they could be near her two brothers, who were attending college in the area. Lucy was also attending college around this time — she was the school's only female student — and in 1847 she moved to Cincinnati, where she enrolled at the Wesleyan Women's College. As such, Lucy would later become the first First Lady to have a college education.

Rutherford kept in contact with Lucy throughout her college years. He was by now living in Cincinnati, where he had opened a law practice. The two were married in December, 1852 at Lucy's home; the groom was eight years older than the bride. Out of the eight children to whom Lucy gave birth, five would survive infancy.

Lucy's anti-slavery stance had a great deal of effect on Rutherford. He rushed off to fight for the North during the Civil War and returned a hero. Lucy also did her share during the War, working a great deal of the time in the army hospital.

After the War, Rutherford was elected Governor of Ohio. Lucy concentrated on helping out the poor and spent a tremendous amount of energy working at the Home for Soldiers' Orphans. In the wake of a close presidential race, Hayes was chosen to be the President in 1877 by a special Congressional commission. As First Lady, Lucy brought a new social conscience to the White House, as well as a more temperate attitude. She banned alcohol at all functions in her new home, dressed in simple clothing, and began the White House traditions of rolling Easter eggs on the White House lawn and keeping a scrapbook which detailed all of the official receptions and dinners. Lucy also supported homes for veterans and the crippled, blind and mentally ill.

In 1881, Lucy and Rutherford retired to their

estate in Fremont, Ohio. Lucy continued to pursue her charitable work and retained her lifelong love of animals — she was one of the first people to own a Siamese cat, just one of her virtual menagerie of animals. In 1889, while watching a tennis match, Lucy died of a massive stroke.

Lucretia Rudolph Garfield
Born: April 19, 1832
Died: March 14, 1918
First Lady: 1881

Lucretia Garfield was raised in the Ohio wilderness by a family devoted to the Disciples of Christ, a religious sect opposed to slavery. Her father, Zebulon Rudolph, was one of the founders of both Hiram College and Arabella Green Mason. She received a solid education at Geauga Seminary, and met her future husband at the school when she was just 17 years old. The two of them became friends, sharing a love of Latin and even starring opposite one another in a class play, but there were no romantic feelings between them at the outset.

After a brief period of separation, they were reunited, by chance, at the Western Reserve

Eclectic Institute in Hiram, Ohio. James Garfield was teaching at the school, and Lucretia was his student. The couple fell in love, but decided to wait to get married until James had a better job. He continued to work hard, and was appointed the President of the school in 1857. The following year, having saved a fair amount of money, he exchanged vows with Lucretia. Over the next few years Lucretia gave birth to three children and conducted research for James while he ran the college. In 1861, despite both his and Lucretia's opposition to war, Garfield joined the Union Army and went off to fight the slavery that he and his wife so despised.

In 1863, James was elected to Congress, and the family began to divide its time between Hiram and Washington. Lucretia spent her days in Washington reading books and raising her children. However, when her husband was elected President in 1880, she was more than happy to take over the duties of First Lady.

Her tenure would be short, however. For only months after moving into the White House, Lucretia contracted malaria and was taken to a retreat in Long Branch, New Jersey. Tragically, on July 2, 1881, while Lucretia was recovering from her illness, James was shot by a crazed assassin. He died two months later.

After briefly living in England with her

daughter, Lucretia returned to Ohio, where she lived a quiet, private life. She died in 1918 in South Pasadena, California, where she had maintained a winter home. Lucretia is buried alongside her family in Lakeview Cemetery.

Ellen Lewis Herndon Arthur

Born: August 30, 1837
Died: January 12, 1880
First Lady: Died before husband took office

Ellen Arthur was born into a Virginia family with an impressive military history. Her father, William Herndon, was a naval officer who was in charge of a mail and passenger ship while on leave from the navy. When the *Central America*, as it was called, went belly up during a storm off Cape Hatteras, Herndon saved his crew and passengers and then went down with his ship. He became a folk hero, and the country provided for Ellen and her mother as a gesture of their appreciation for William's bravery.

While Ellen was not surrounded by wealth as a child, she did not lack for much, and was even taken on a tour of Europe by her uncle — the head of the United States Naval Observatory in Washington — when she was 16 years old. She met her future husband, Chester A. Arthur, when she and her mother moved to New York after the death of her father. Arthur was a successful lawyer at the time, and he was impressed by Ellen's intelligence and cheerful demeanor.

The couple married in October, 1859, and settled in with Ellen's mother. Arthur continued his career as a lawyer, and soon began to make his name known in the political field as well. Ellen had a son in December, 1860, but the child died before his third birthday. She would later give birth to another son and a daughter, both of whom would live well into the 20th century.

As Chester's career continued to blossom, Ellen took on the duties of entertaining with a great deal of relish. She helped organize the Mendelssohn Glee Club and displayed her beautiful contralto voice as one of their soloists. The Club took up a good deal of her time, as they performed concerts all over the city.

In 1878, Ellen's mother passed away, and Ellen suffered severe depression, from which she never fully recovered. Within two years she would fall ill, dying of pneumonia at the age of 42 on January 12, 1880. Two days earlier she had attended a benefit concert and caught cold while waiting for her carriage to arrive. Chester became President the following year when James Garfield died from an assassin's bullet.

Frances Folsom Cleveland

Born: July 21, 1864
Died: October 29, 1947
First Lady: 1886-1889; 1893-1897

When Emma Folsom gave birth to her first daughter, her husband's 27-year-old friend and partner hurried over to the house to see the new baby. It was undoubtedly the first and only time that a future President would meet his future wife when she was a newborn baby. Grover Cleveland would become Frances Folsom's favorite "uncle" during her childhood — he even bought her first baby carriage — and when Emma's father died when she was 11 years old, "Uncle Cleve" would become her guardian and closest confidant.

While Grover's career took him all over the state of New York — from Sheriff of Erie County to Mayor of Buffalo to Governor of New York — he stayed in touch with Emma throughout her childhood and teenage years. He often sent her roses while she was away at college in Aurora, and a little over a year after he was elected President, he proposed to Emma. At the time of their marriage in June of 1886, Grover was 49 years old, and the blue-eyed Emma was one month shy of her 22nd birthday.

The entire nation, which had been waiting eagerly for the most eligible bachelor in the land to find a mate, went crazy. The gossip pages were filled with the smallest details of Cleveland's wedding, honeymoon, and return to Washington. Frances became an extremely popular First Lady, and women around the country copied her fashion sense — which included her refusal to wear a bustle — and her hair style. When she held open house days at the White House, thousands of people would wait in line for hours just to shake her hand. Afterwards, Frances would often have her arms massaged to relieve the pain caused by shaking so many hands.

When it came time for Cleveland's reelection campaign, the posters prominently featured a photograph of Frances alongside her husband. Grover lost the race, but Frances remained upbeat, proclaiming that they would be back in four years. It was a promise that was kept, for in 1892 Cleveland recaptured the White House, and the couple returned to Washington. Another four years of parties and receptions followed, as Frances reestablished herself as an exceedingly popular First Lady. During this period Frances gave birth to her second daughter, Esther — her first daughter, Ruth had been born in between presidential terms. (The popular legend that the Baby Ruth candy bar was named for Ruth Cleveland is false.) Esther is the only child of a President to be born in the White House. Another daughter, Marion, was born two years later.

At the end of Grover's second term, the couple retired to Princeton, New Jersey. Frances gave birth to two more sons. Unfortunately, in 1904, Ruth died of diphtheria at the age of 12. In 1909, Grover himself passed away, the victim of a heart attack. Frances remained in Princeton, and even married a Princeton archeology professor in 1913. She got involved in charity work, and worked for her alma mater, Wells College. She was also the President of the Needlework Guild of America, which distributed millions of garments during the depression. She died in Baltimore while visiting her son on his 50th birthday. She was 83.

Caroline Lavinia Scott Harrison
Born: October 10, 1832
Died: October 25, 1889
First Lady: 1889-1893

Caroline Harrison was born and raised in Oxford, Ohio. Her father, Rev. Dr. John Witherspoon Scott, was the founder and president of Oxford Seminary and a teacher at Miami University. As such, Caroline received an excellent education. Caroline and Benjamin Harrison met when they were both teenagers — he was a student at Miami University. It was love at first sight.

After Harrison finished college, they were married in October, 1853. Young and poor, they initially lived at the home of Benjamin's father in North Bend, Ohio. Benjamin pursued the study of law during this period, and was admitted to the bar in 1854. The couple moved to Indianapolis, where Benjamin was able to use his politically potent name to gain a position with a well-regarded law firm. The couple had three children, one of whom was stillborn.

After gaining prominence in the Civil War, Benjamin came home and continued his career while Caroline worked with the First Presbyterian Church and pursued her interest in needlework and painting (she was an accomplished watercolor artist). In 1880, Benjamin was elected Senator. Despite his fame, the arrogant Harrison was not well-liked. Fortunately, Caroline could make friends at the drop of a hat, and she was able to help Benjamin overcome his problems at the social level. She charmed the people in Washington when the couple arrived in 1881, which in turn enabled Harrison to continue his rise in the political arena.

After recovering from several years of illness, Caroline was ready and willing to take over as First Lady when she and her husband entered the White House in 1889. The executive mansion was immediately filled with children and grandchildren, and a festive atmosphere prevailed. Caroline oversaw a total overhaul of the by now run-down White House. She erected the first White House Christmas tree, replaced the White House china with a pattern of her own design, and was elected as the first president-general of the Daughters of the American Revolution when the Sons of the American Revolution refused to admit her because she was a woman. Likewise, she agreed to support Johns Hopkins Medical School under the condition that women would be given equal admittance.

During Benjamin's run for a second term, Caroline contracted tuberculosis. Both Harrison and Grover Cleveland postponed their campaigns while Caroline went to the Adirondacks in an attempt to recover from her illness. But it was not to be — she died on October 25, 1892. Thousands turned out as her coffin was carried through the streets of Washington on the way to the train station. She was buried in Indianapolis in the Harrison family plot. Her husband would join her there some eight years later.

Ida Saxton McKinley

Born: June 8, 1847
Died: May 26, 1907
First Lady: 1897-1901

Not much is known about Ida McKinley's childhood. She grew up in Canton, Ohio, and her father was a wealthy banker. She apparently received an excellent education at Miss Sandford's in Cleveland, Ohio, and Miss Eastman's Brooke Hall Seminary in Media, Pennsylvania. At the age of 22, she traveled throughout Europe with her sister, Mary "Pina."

The auburn-haired Ida had a reputation as being exceedingly headstrong and egotistical. When she set her sights on something, she would go out of her way to make sure that she got it. William McKinley would be such a target.

She had first met McKinley at a family picnic at Meyer's Lake when she was 20 years old. Nothing much happened until she came upon him again a few years later when she was working at her father's bank in Canton and he was a well-known attorney in the same area. Ida evidently saw the mark of greatness in McKinley, and went after him with a vengeance. He, in turn, was flattered, and fell madly in love with her. They were married on January 25, 1871.

They were given a home by Ida's father as a wedding present, and Ida bore a daughter on the day of their first anniversary. Tragedy, however, was beginning to rear its ugly head. First, Ida's mother died. Then, Ida suffered through an enormously difficult second pregnancy. Among her suspected ailments were brain damage, epilepsy, and phlebitis. The second child, a daughter, died only five months after being born, further throwing Ida's mental and physical health into jeopardy. By the time she was 26, Ida was often confined to her bed and was in need of constant medical attention. Her health worsened when her first daughter died several months shy of her fourth birthday. Ida began regularly suffering from epileptic seizures and migraine headaches.

Amazingly, William was able to continue his remarkable political career despite the enormous amount of time he spent caring for his wife. From Congressman to Governor to President, he remained unfailingly devoted to her. Ida's health fluctuated from bad to good, and William was always eager to pay for any cure that was presented to them.

At McKinley's Inaugural Ball, Ida suffered a seizure and had to be whisked away. William himself took her home, going to bed early while the celebration continued without him or his wife. For the most part, Ida was not able to perform her duties as First Lady, although there were a few events here and there that she was well enough to organize and preside over.

William died from an assassin's bullet in September, 1901. Ida returned to their home in Canton, Ohio and lived for another six years, during which time she visited William's grave on a daily basis. When she died she was buried next to William and their two daughters.

Edith Kermit Carow Roosevelt

Born: August 6, 1861
Died: September 30, 1948
First Lady: 1901-1909

Edith and Theodore Roosevelt spent nearly all of their lives together. They first met when she was an infant and he was three years old. Throughout her childhood, Edith's best friend was Theodore's younger sister, Corinne. The Carrow home was located on Union Square in New York City, right next door to where Theodore's grandparents lived. Indeed, even as young children, Theodore and Edith realized that they loved each other and would probably marry one day.

However, at some point during their teenage years, Theodore and Edith had a terrible fight and the two went their separate ways — he to Harvard and she to a private school for girls in Manhattan. In 1880, Theodore married Alice Hathaway Lee, and a heartbroken Edith attended the wedding. Theodore and Alice had a child in 1884, but two days later, on Valentine's Day, tragedy struck: in a matter of hours, Theodore lost both his 22-year-old wife and his 49-year-old mother.

Another year would pass before Theodore and the statuesque Edith would see or speak to each other. Finally, in the fall of 1885, they accidentally saw each other while they were both visiting his sister's home. All of their old feelings were rekindled and they fell in love again. They were married in London at St. George's Church in December of 1886.

Edith faced the task of raising a step-daughter and living in the home Theodore had originally built for his former wife. She kept a stiff upper lip about the situation however, and went on with her life bravely. While Theodore concentrated on his career, Edith managed the household finances and raised her step-daughter and the five children that she would go on to have with Theodore.

When Roosevelt was elected President in 1901, Edith managed to pack up the entire household and organize the move to Washington. Under Theodore and Edith, the White House was a much more informal place than it had been in previous administrations. Children and friends of the family roamed the halls, playing practical jokes and having a grand old time. It was (and will most likely be) the only time the White House saw an alligator in a bath tub, horses in the elevators, and snakes in the entry hall. Casual lunches and dinners replaced the more formal receptions other Presidents and their wives had traditionally hosted. Perhaps Edith's longest lasting contribution as First Lady was her thorough restoration of the White House, for which she spent nearly five hundred thousand dollars of the government's money.

After Theodore's term ended, the Roosevelt's retired to their home in Oyster Bay. In 1911, Edith was thrown off of a horse and lapsed into a coma for nine days. Because of this incident, she lost her sense of taste and smell. Theodore died on January 6, 1919. Edith lived for nearly 30 years after the death of her dear husband. She lost three of her sons in the two World Wars. Edith did not waste away with grief, however, but chose to forge on, traveling around the world — she referred to her journeys as "Odyssey of a Grandmother" — and doing charitable work. During Prohibition she continued to serve alcohol because she felt that Congress should not dictate personal habits. She passed away at the age of 87.

Helen Herron Taft

Born: September 2, 1861
Died: May 22, 1943
First Lady: 1909-1913

In spite of the fact that the Herron family and the Taft family knew each other quite well, the clans were so large — the Herron's had 11 children, the Taft's had 10 — that Helen Herron and William Howard Taft did not meet until she was 18 and he was 22. Both were born and raised in Cincinnati, Ohio. Helen was given a solid education and spent a great deal of her childhood practicing the piano. One of the highlights of her childhood was when Lucy Hayes invited Helen to visit the White House (Helen's father was a law partner of Rutherford B. Hayes). Helen was so enthralled with Washington during this trip that she made it one of her life-long goals to return there one day.

Helen finally met William at a sledding party on Mt. Auburn near the Taft home; apparently, Helen was more impressed by William than he was by her. Their friendship continued on a very informal basis for several years, and Helen took a job as a teacher in a private Cincinnati school. William finally came around, however, and, after a bit of resistance from Helen (she rejected two of his proposals), who had evidently grown weary of waiting for William to consider her for his wife, the two of them were married in June of 1886. It had been seven years since their first meeting.

Setting a pattern of world travel that would mark the remainder of their lives, the newlyweds took off on a one hundred day journey to Europe. When they returned, they settled in Cincinnati and William was soon appointed to the Supreme Court of Ohio — quite an honor for a 29-year-old. Helen, however, wanted more. She had her sights set on Washington, and when President Harrison appointed Taft as the Solicitor General of the United States, Helen, William, and their three children moved to the Capitol. Two years later however, in 1892, the Tafts returned to Cincinnati when Harrison appointed William to the Federal Circuit Court in Ohio. Helen was not pleased with this change, but she made the best of it. Pursuing her love of music, she co-founded the Cincinnati Symphony Orchestra Association, soliciting money from her friends and relatives.

In 1900, President McKinley called upon William to help establish a government in the Philippines. Helen, seeing this as a possible step towards bigger and better things, urged her husband to accept the post, and the family headed off to the islands. They would remain there for four exceedingly happy years, so happy, in fact, that when President Roosevelt offered Taft a seat on the Supreme Court, he turned it down, preferring to stay in the Philippines. In 1904, however, Roosevelt wanted Taft to become the Secretary of War. It was a position that both Helen and William felt he could not refuse, one that had the potential to lead to the presidency. Their strategy paid off in 1909, when William was elected to the highest office in the land.

From the moment of her husband's inauguration, Helen made her presence felt in the White House, constantly letting her opinions be heard and rebuking William whenever she felt the need. She even rode in a limousine with her husband during the inaugural parade — the first First Lady to do so. Less than three months into her term as First Lady, however, Helen suffered a debilitating stroke. She could not speak for many months and essentially had to learn to talk again. Remarkably, she experienced a nearly one hundred percent recovery, a small speech impairment being the only thing that would linger on for the remainder of her life.

Helen was the first First Lady to attend cabinet meetings — supposedly to keep the narcoleptic President from falling asleep. Helen's legacy in Washington, however, is the thousands of Yoshino cherry trees she had planted around the city's Tidal Basin. These beautiful cherry blossoms are still widely visible today. Perhaps the biggest social event during the Taft's four-year term was the couple's silver anniversary, for which thousands of people showed up. It should also be noted that William and Helen were the first presidential couple to ride in an automobile on a regular basis.

At the end of Taft's presidential term, the couple moved to New Haven, Connecticut, where William taught law at Yale University. Helen led a quiet life during this time, writing her memoirs and proudly celebrating the moment when her daughter became the dean of

Bryn Mawr University. In 1921, William was offered the Chief Justice of the U.S. Supreme Court, and thus became the only man to ever serve as both President and Chief Justice. He would preside over the Court for a little more than eight years, until his death in 1930. Helen remained in Washington, until she passed away some 22 years later, just shy of her 83rd birthday.

Ellen Louise Axson Wilson

Born: May 15, 1860
Died: August 6, 1914
First Lady: 1913-1914

Ellen Wilson was born and raised in Georgia, and was the recipient of a rather strict upbringing from her father, who was a third generation Presbyterian minister. She was taught to observe the social customs of the old South as well and worship the Lord above. When Ellen's mother passed away in 1883, Ellen found herself having to care for not only her devastated father, but her two brothers and one sister as well. She was 22 years old at the time.

Later that year, Woodrow Wilson stopped off in Rome on some business, and while attending a Church service he spotted Ellen and immediately fell in love with her. He arranged a meeting, and the two corresponded regularly over the next few months. In September of that same year, Woodrow proposed to Ellen, and she readily accepted. Marriage, however, would have to wait. Woodrow wanted to finish his studies at John Hopkins University, and Ellen still had the overwhelming responsibility of taking care of her father and her brothers. But after Mr. Axson passed away in May of 1884, Ellen was able to concentrate on her own life. Her older brother had by now gone off to college, and she sent her younger brother to live with relatives. Instead of rushing off to marry Woodrow, however, Ellen decided to pursue her interest in art, and enrolled in the Art Students' League in New York.

Woodrow, in the meantime, had experienced a great deal of success with a book he had written, and he persuaded Ellen that the time was right for them to wed. On June 24, 1885, Ellen and Woodrow were married at her grandfather's home in Savannah, Georgia.

The first fifteen years of their marriage were marked by a great deal of moving around, as Woodrow accepted one educational position after another — including the presidency of Princeton University. During this period, Ellen gave birth to three children. In 1910, Woodrow won election as the Governor of New Jersey, and two years later he was elected President of the United States.

The Wilson's time in the White House was dominated by family matters. While the usual receptions and dinners still took place, the marriages of their children highlighted the social calendar of their first two years in Washington. Ellen managed to pursue her love for painting, even going so far as to construct an art studio on the third floor of the White House. She also spent a good deal of her time proofreading Wilson's books, articles, and speeches, and was a member of the Board of Associated Charities as well.

By the summer of 1914, Ellen was suffering from Bright's disease (a kidney disease), and in August of that year she passed away at the age of 54. Her funeral services were conducted in the identical church where Woodrow had seen her some 31 years earlier.

Edith Bolling Galt Wilson

Born: October 15, 1872
Died: December 28, 1961
First Lady: 1915-1921

Edith Wilson was a direct descendant of Pocahonas. The Bolling family had a long and distinguished history in Virginia, continued by Edith's father, who was a circuit court judge. Edith's childhood years were spent around the home, where she was educated by her grandmother, who taught her how to read, write and speak French. She was later able to spend two years in private school, but her father forced her to withdraw because he could not afford to pay for the education of both Edith — who had a photographic memory — and her brothers, and felt it was more important for the boys to receive schooling.

While visiting her sister in Washington in 1880, Edith met Norman Galt, who came from a wealthy family. Norman fell in love with Edith, and through a great deal of persistence, finally persuaded her to marry him. Two years later, a pregnant Edith had a miscarriage and was never able to have children again. When Norman died suddenly in 1908, Edith inherited his fortune, including the popular jewelry store that he owned.

After traveling throughout Europe for several years, Edith returned home to Washington. One day her friend, Alice Gordon, invited her to the White House. Alice was dating Admiral Cary Grayson, the President's physician, at the time. From the moment Edith entered the White House and was introduced to Woodrow Wilson, the recently widowed President was smitten.

Woodrow and Edith began a quiet romance. The election of 1916 was on the horizon, and the President's advisors worried that the public would not accept his dating so soon after his wife had died. Edith agreed, and so the President and his new love became secretly engaged but postponed their wedding plans until after the election. Their first public appearance together was at a World Series baseball game between the Philadelphia Athletics and the Boston Red Sox. The gossip continued to spread, and ultimately the President decided to throw caution to the wind, and on December 18, 1915, he married Edith in a quiet ceremony. The public, far from being shocked, was actually quite enthusiastic about the marriage, and Edith triumphantly took her place as the nation's First Lady.

When the United States entered the War in 1917, Edith proudly set an example for the rest of the country by cutting down on the number of receptions and dinners in the White House, and by forgoing gasoline, meat, wheat, and heat on certain days of the week. She arranged for such Hollywood stars as Charlie Chaplin and Mary Pickford to sell Liberty Bonds, and sewed clothing for the Red Cross. Edith also had sheep graze on the White House lawn and then sold the wool to support the War.

When the War ended, Woodrow, exhausted from his attempt to gain support for his League of Nations proposal, fell ill and woke up one day to find himself paralyzed. The news of the President's health was kept a secret, however, and Edith effectively took over the daily running of the presidency! Nobody knows for certain how long this charade lasted — estimates vary from six weeks to seventeen months. At some point, Woodrow recovered enough to resume his duties, but Edith remained close by for the remainder of his term.

In 1921, Woodrow and Edith left the White House but chose to stay in Washington. Woodrow would only live for three more years, however. After spending a year in seclusion, Edith traveled around the world. In 1939, she published her autobiography, *My Memoir*. She served as a director of the Woodrow Wilson Foundation, helped to dedicate the Woodrow Wilson National Shrine, was a participant in the 1956 Woodrow Wilson Centennial Celebration, and regularly attended League of Nations' meetings. Edith remained alive long enough to be present at the 1961 inauguration of John F. Kennedy. She died in December of that year. The Washington D.C. home where she lived for four decades is today a national museum.

Florence Kling Harding

Born: August 15, 1860
Died: November 21, 1924
First Lady: 1921-1923

Florence Harding was born into a wealthy family in Marion, Ohio. Her father was a banker, and the Kling home was widely regarded as the most extravagant in town. Unfortunately, inside of the home there existed a great deal of unhappiness. Florence's parents often fought, and there was very little love to go around. Florence argued with her father on a regular basis, and she was never very fond of her two brothers.

After taking courses at the Cincinnati Conservatory of Music, Florence returned home and sought out the affections of the young men in town. When she was 19, she eloped with her next door neighbor, Henry DeWolfe; six months later, their son was born. Henry was essentially a loser. He did not want to get a job, and Florence's father, angry at her for the situation she had gotten herself into, refused to help the struggling couple. Two years after they had wed, Henry walked out and never returned. Florence officially divorced him in 1886, and allowed her father to adopt her little boy.

When Florence met Warren Harding, she

was giving piano lessons to, among others, Harding's sister, and he was publishing a struggling newspaper called the *Marion Star*. The two of them fell in love and, despite her father's physical threats, were married in July of 1891. At the time, Florence was 30 years old and Warren was 5 years her junior. The stubborn, somewhat masculine Florence most certainly wore the pants in the family, and on more than one occasion nearly drove Warren to have a nervous breakdown. In 1894, she sent Warren to a sanitarium and took over control of the newspaper. While he was away, she turned the paper into a profitable operation.

Upon his release from the sanitarium, Warren continued to allow Florence to run the *Star* while he pursued a career in politics. He quickly went from County Auditor to state Senator to Lieutenant Governor of Ohio. In 1905, Florence underwent a kidney operation, and would never really be in good health again. While Warren looked after her every need, he found himself becoming involved with other women.

In 1914, Harding was elected to the U.S. Senate, and the couple moved to Washington. Warren found it easy to get along with the men in the town, but Florence had some difficulty with the women. Nevertheless, the couple climbed up the social and political ladder, and in 1920 Harding was elected President.

While the aristocracy may not have taken too kindly to the Hardings, the public loved them. Florence proclaimed herself and her husband to be "plain folks," and would often personally greet tourists who were visiting the White House. The couple entertained on a nightly basis, and Florence was known to visit with nearly anyone who cared to call on her. She was also famous for her love of gardening, and even has some varieties of roses and sweet peas named after her.

After catching her husband with another woman, Florence and Warren often had loud, bitter arguments. She found solace working with injured soldiers at VA hospitals. The couple took an exhausting trip around the country in 1923 in an attempt to boost the public's confidence in Harding's scandal-ridden administration. The tour proved to be too much for Warren, however, and he died in San Francisco after catching pneumonia on the journey from Alaska to California. There has been some speculation that Florence poisoned Harding because she was tired of his adulterous ways, and because she wanted to spare him the embarrassment of the forthcoming Teapot Dome scandal. Florence would survive Warren by little more than a year, succumbing to kidney failure at the age of 64.

Grace Anna Goodhue Coolidge
Born: January 3, 1879
Died: July 8, 1957
First Lady: 1923-1929

Grace Coolidge, an only child, was born and raised in Burlington, Vermont. Her father was a steamboat inspector who worked on nearby Lake Champlain.

After graduating from the University of Vermont in 1902, Grace found a job teaching at the Clarke Institute for the Deaf in Northhampton, Massachusetts. One day, while looking out of her window, she spotted a soldier in a bathroom across the way shaving in his uniform with a straw hat on his head. The sight struck her as being very funny and she let out a loud laugh. Calvin Coolidge took the episode in stride, and when he was later introduced to her, he merely explained that he had kept his hat on in order to keep some wayward locks of hair in place. The couple was married a few years later and settled down in Northhampton where Calvin had a modest law practice. They would have two sons together.

Calvin's political career began to blossom, and by 1918 he was elected as Governor of Massachusetts. Grace, meanwhile, had kept herself extremely busy within the community of Northhampton, and had at one point been elected national President of the Pi Beta Phi fraternity she had joined while in college. A good deal of Calvin's political success can be attributed to Grace as well, for in contrast to the closed-mouth and rather uninspiring future President, Grace was lively and well-liked by all.

When Coolidge took over the presidency in the wake of Harding's death in 1923, Grace was immediately welcomed with open arms by all levels of society. Men were amazed by her astounding knowledge and love for the game of baseball, and women found her taste in clothing to be first rate.

Tragedy, however, struck Warren and Grace at the end of their first year in the White House. Their son, 16-year-old Calvin Jr., died of an infection. He had been playing tennis without socks and the resulting blister on his foot turned septic. When Calvin won election to a full term in November, 1924, the Coolidge's elation was tempered by the grief they were still feeling in the wake of their son's sudden death.

The next four years were largely uneventful. Coolidge did not allow his wife to speak in public and maintained tight control over how she dressed, how she wore her hair, and in what activities she could and could not participate. Grace, displaying her love for music and the theater, did manage to invite such performers as Sergei Rachmaninoff, Al Jolson, and Will Rogers to the White House, and in 1927 the President and his First Lady paid a personal tribute to Charles Lindbergh.

Calvin's retirement would not last long, for he passed away in early 1933, a little less than four years after leaving office. Grace resumed her work with the deaf, helping to make the Clarke Institute one of the finest educational centers in the country. Among those who worked with her were Helen Keller and Spencer Tracy. After living a long and full life, she passed away in 1957 at the age of 78.

Lou Henry Hoover

Born: March 29, 1875
Died: January 7, 1944
First Lady: 1929-1933

Lou Hoover spent the early years of her childhood playing in the wilderness that surrounded her Waterloo, Iowa home. She rode horses, hunted, and studied the geology of the area. At the age of 10, the extremely athletic girl moved with her family to Whittier, California, where she was introduced to the beliefs of the

Quakers. Six years later, the family moved up the coast to Monterey. She finished high school and began preparing for a career as a teacher. However, in the summer of 1894, Lou heard a lecture on geology which rekindled her interest in the subject. Lou subsequently decided to enroll at Stanford to study geology; she was the sole female in her class.

During her freshman year, a professor at the university introduced Lou to fellow student Herbert Hoover. The two of them began to date, and when Herbert graduated that June, they agreed that they would one day be married. Lou herself graduated a few years later in 1898. At the time, Herbert had received an offer to work as an engineer for the Chinese Engineering and Mining Company. He proposed to Lou and asked her to move to the Orient with him. She happily consented, and they were married on January 31, 1899.

The next decade was a period of great adventure. The Hoovers traveled from continent to continent as Herbert was offered and accepted a variety of mining jobs. During this time, Lou gave birth to two sons. She also helped Herbert write his classic book, *Principles of Mining*, and translated a book from Latin which won her the Mining and Metallurgical Award. The years of World War I saw both Lou, who could speak five languages, and Herbert working for a variety of relief organizations; she even served as the President of the Society of American Women in London, and was an executive member of the American Women's War Relief Fund and Hospital. By 1921, Herbert was asked by President Harding to be his Secretary of Commerce, and the Hoovers moved to Washington D.C. Lou, who had become involved with the Girl Scouts during the War, became their national President in 1922. In 1923, she was selected as the Vice President of the NCAA.

When Herbert took over the presidency in 1929, Lou immediately set about renovating the White House, and paid for the majority of the changes out of her and her husband's own funds. The couple did a great deal of entertaining — both formal and informal — and hosted receptions for Kings and Queens from around the world.

After Hoover lost to Roosevelt in the 1932 election, the couple divided their time between their home in Palo Alto, California and an apartment in New York City's Waldorf Towers. With the outbreak of World War II, the Hoovers once again found themselves busy working with a variety of relief organizations, including the YMCA, the League of Women Voters and the Salvation Army. As the War neared an end, however, Lou realized that she had been going at too hard of a pace. She felt extremely tired and decided to go back to Palo Alto to rest. When she returned to New York a few months later, she was still not well. On January 7, 1944, she suffered a heart attack and died. One thousand people showed up at her funeral service at St. Bartholomew's Church in New York City.

Anna Eleanor Roosevelt Roosevelt
Born: October 11, 1884
Died: November 7, 1962
First Lady: 1933-1945

The most admired First Lady of them all was born into one of the most socially respected families in American history: the Roosevelts (she and Franklin were distant cousins). In fact, one of her mother's ancestors delivered the oath of office to George Washington. Other ancestors signed the Declaration of Independence.

Eleanor's mother, with whom she was never very close, died when Eleanor was only eight years old. The young girl had an extremely good relationship with her father, but he was an alcoholic and he passed away in a sanitarium only two years later. Thus, Eleanor, for much of her childhood, was raised by her grandmother, who tended to dress her in old fashioned clothing and refused to allow her to play with children her own age.

The shy and homely looking girl was educated by a series of tutors until the age of 15, when she enrolled at a private girls' school near London. Her experience in London was an extremely happy one, and Eleanor finally emerged from her shell. She returned full of confidence to New York at the age of 18 and began dating Franklin, who was at the time attending Harvard University. They were married on St. Patrick's Day of 1905, and Eleanor's uncle, Theodore, gave the bride away. Eleanor and Franklin would have six children together.

During the early years of their marriage, Eleanor had to constantly battle Franklin's mother, Sara, for control of her own family. Even as Franklin's political career forged ahead and the couple moved away from New York City to Albany and then to Washington, Sara still made her presence felt. In 1921, when Franklin became paralyzed after taking a swim in a freezing bay, Sara wanted to put him in a wheel chair and essentially make him a prisoner of her home, with servants at his disposal 24 hours a day. Eleanor finally put her foot down. She knew that Franklin still had plenty of challenges and accomplishments ahead of him. Over the next few years, Eleanor helped Franklin learn how to walk with the aid of crutches and then a cane. She encouraged him to continue to pursue his political ambitions, and shared his joy when he was elected Governor of New York in 1928.

By the time of Roosevelt's presidential victory in 1932, Eleanor was an integral part of Franklin's political team. She gave him advice and took on important jobs that essentially improved the plight of the homeless, the disabled, African-Americans, and women. As First Lady, she performed all of the duties, such as entertaining, that were expected of her, and much, much more. She wrote a popular newspaper column, appeared on numerous radio programs, and gave lectures across the country. During World War II, Eleanor visited troops overseas, flying over five hundred thousand miles during this period, and gathered vital information which she would share with her husband upon her return.

After Franklin's sudden death in 1945, Eleanor continued her busy schedule. In 1946, President Truman appointed her as an American delegate to the United Nations. During her stint in the U.N., she became known as a champion of human rights. She also continued to write and lecture on a variety of topics, and served on the boards of the NAACP and the Americans for Democratic Action. In November, 1962, her tremendous energy finally failed her and she passed away. She was buried next to Franklin in the rose garden in Hyde Park.

Elizabeth (Bess) Virginia Wallace Truman
Born: February 13, 1885
Died: October 18, 1982
First Lady: 1945-1953

Bess Truman was quite a tomboy as a child. She loved playing with the boys, and excelled at shot-putting, basketball, ice skating, baseball, and such outdoor sports as fishing and hunting. Reportedly, she was the only girl in Independence, Missouri who could whistle through her teeth!

She first met Harry Truman when they were both small children. They remained friends through the years, but Harry did not hold much interest for Bess — no matter how much he claimed he was in love with her. Harry was not particularly good looking, and his eye problems forced him to wear glasses and precluded him from engaging in any of the physical activities that Bess so loved. Besides, blue-eyed Bess, as one of the most popular girls in town, had many suitors who seemed much better qualified as a potential husband than did Harry Truman.

Bess's father died when she was 18 years old. For the next two years, she helped her mother take care of her three brothers. Not much is known about Bess Wallace's life during the next decade. A boy she was dating died under mysterious circumstances in 1910, and Bess has always remained tight-lipped about this event as well as her life during the years that followed. What is known is that by 1914, Harry Truman was dating Bess on a regular basis. In 1917, Bess finally agreed to marry Harry, but the wedding would have to wait until he finished serving in the army during World War I. They were finally married on June 28, 1919, some 29 years after they had first met. In February, 1924, Bess would give birth to her first and only child, a daughter named Margaret.

Harry's political career began in 1922 when he became involved with the Pendergast family, who were the Democratic head honchos of Kansas City. In 1934, Harry became a junior U.S. Senator and the Trumans moved to Washington. Bess went to work for Harry as a secretary, setting a pattern that would continue throughout the remainder of Harry's career — he would rarely make an important decision without first consulting his wife.

When Truman became President in 1945, Bess angered the press corps by retaining a firm grip on her privacy. She would not hold press conferences, and went about living her life in a quiet manner, avoiding calling attention to herself at all costs. Bess did her own shopping, made the beds, and addressed her own Christmas cards.

In 1948, the Trumans moved to the Blair House while the White House was completely gutted and rebuilt at a cost of nearly six million dollars. They would not return to the newly redone White House until the last year of Truman's second term in office. When it came time to leave Washington, Bess and Harry returned to their beloved hometown of Independence. Bess rejoined her bridge club, took regular trips to the local library, and resumed shopping at the local supermarket. Harry oversaw the building of the Harry S. Truman Library. After years of quiet domesticity, the longest living First Lady passed away at the age of 97.

Mamie Geneva Doud Eisenhower

Born: November 14, 1896
Died: November 1, 1979
First Lady: 1953-1961

Mamie Geneva Doud Eisenhower was the last First Lady to be born during the 19th century. Originally from Cedar Rapids, Iowa, she soon moved with her family to Colorado Springs, Colorado, then to Denver. Ultimately, the family would divide their time between Denver and San Antonio, Texas. This vagabond lifestyle would continue in her adult years, when she would move 27 times in 37 years with her husband, Dwight David Eisenhower. It wasn't until her eight years in the White House that Mamie would truly be able to settle down.

The petite, vivacious, and out-going Mamie first met Ike in 1915 while she was visiting Fort Sam Houston near San Antonio. Ike spotted her as she toured the fort, and when their eyes met their fate was sealed; they were married less than a year later. Their first child, nicknamed "Icky," was born in September of 1917. Three years later, Icky contracted scarlet fever and passed away. A second son, John Sheldon Doud Eisenhower, was born during the summer of 1922. The years surrounding his birth were marked by a great deal of moving from army post to army post, including a two year stay in Panama. Between 1924 and 1941, they would live around the world in such diverse places as Paris, the Philippines, and Washington, D.C. In Manila, their apartment was nicknamed Club Eisenhower because of the fantastic parties they threw.

During World War II, Ike began his rise to prominence; by the end of the War, he was the Supreme Commander of the Allied Expeditionary Force and his name was known around the world. Such important posts as the Chief of Staff, President of Columbia University, and Commander of NATO forces followed, and with these positions came new homes in new cities. For the two years before Ike would take over the presidency, the Eisenhowers lived in a luxurious villa outside of Paris.

The couple's long run in the White House was marked by lavish receptions for some of the most important people in the world, from the King and Queen of Greece, to Prince Philip and Queen Elizabeth, to Nikita Khrushchev. Mamie stayed out of Ike's political affairs, choosing instead to concentrate on the more domestic duties of the First Lady. She had a reputation for being an incredibly meticulous housekeeper, to the point where she didn't like to see footprints on the carpeting. When Ike fell ill in 1955, thousands of sympathy cards and letters poured in from around the country and Mamie answered every one of them in turquoise ink.

When the Eisenhower's stay in the White House came to an end, they retired to a beautiful farmhouse in Gettysburg. Ike became ill once again, and Mamie moved into the Walter Reed Army Hospital to be with him. After Ike's death in 1969, Mamie traveled to Europe to visit her son, who was then living in Belgium. She later returned to her farm in Gettysburg where she spent her last years living quietly in the serene environment. In 1977, she helped christen the USS *Dwight D. Eisenhower*. She died in 1979.

Jacqueline Lee Bouvier Kennedy Onassis
Born: July 28, 1929
First Lady: 1961-1963

The first First Lady to be born in the 20th century was raised in Manhattan and in a tony section of Long Island. Her mother and father were both from leading families, and Jackie had all the advantages that come along with being born into high society. She received press coverage at the age of two when she entered her dog in a show, and this fascination by the media has continued to the present day. By the age of five she was riding in horse shows, and by the age of eleven she had won dozens of prizes, including a double championship. Educated at the finest schools New York had to offer, Jackie was a bright student who reportedly read a collection of short stories by Anton Chekhov at the age of six.

When the Depression wreaked havoc with her family's fortune, her parents, perhaps feeling financial pressure for the first time, divorced. Her mother soon remarried, however, and Jackie's step-father, Hugh Auchincloss, was much wealthier than her father. Instead of vacationing in the Hamptons, Jackie now spent her summers in the Newport area. By now, Jackie had grown into a beautiful and accomplished young lady who was fluent in French, Spanish, and Latin. Her boundless creativity was especially apparent in her ability to act, paint and write. In 1947, she was proclaimed "Queen Debutante of the Year" by society columnist Cholly Knickerbocker.

Jackie attended college at Vassar and the Sorbonne in Paris, and graduated from George Washington University with a degree in art. She first met John F. Kennedy while interviewing the young Senator for the *Washington Times Herald*, and the two started dating in mid-1951

(Jackie was seen on JFK's arm at the Eisenhower inauguration). Their romance was slow in developing, but things finally heated up and they were married, in what was surely the social event of the year, in September, 1953.

Her life as a Kennedy was much like her childhood: there were fabulous summer homes, plenty of horses to ride, and glitzy functions to attend. While life had been relatively easy for Jackie, pregnancy proved to be an entirely different matter. In 1955, she had a miscarriage, and the next year her baby was stillborn. She gave birth to Caroline and John, Jr. in 1957 and 1960 respectively, but her last child, Patrick, lived for only two days.

When John Kennedy was elected President, Jackie immediately brought a new sense of style and elegance to the White House. Women across the country rushed to beauty parlors to copy her hairdo, and flooded stores to buy clothes that matched the fashions the new First Lady tended to prefer. Jackie's interest in the arts benefited such performers as Pablo Casals and Isaac Stern, both of whom made appearances in the White House. Whenever the couple traveled, they were greeted by enthusiastic throngs of well-wishers. In 1962, over 50 million people tuned in to watch Jackie conduct a television tour of the White House; she had redecorated the showplace with furnishings that represented different periods throughout the history of the United States.

Jackie's incredible show of strength in the wake of the Kennedy assassination helped the people of our nation get through some of its darkest days. It was her idea to have the eternal flame burn next to JFK's grave. She attempted to return to the life of a private citizen, but the press and public would not allow this to happen. Her home became a tourist attraction and her every move was reported and analyzed. When she married Aristotle Onassis in 1968, there was a negative uproar by the public at large. It seemed that Jackie was expected to grieve forever, instead of getting on with her life. Aristotle Onassis died in 1975. Jackie is currently busy working as a book editor.

Claudia Taylor (Lady Bird) Johnson
Born: December 12, 1912
First Lady: 1963-1969

Born and raised in Texas, Claudia Taylor would live in the same house, known as "Brick House," until she married Lyndon Johnson. She acquired her nickname, "Lady Bird," from a nanny, who reportedly said about her, "She's purty as a ladybird." Lady Bird's mother died when the future First Lady was not yet six years old. From this point on, she was raised by her Aunt Effie. It was through her Aunt that Lady Bird learned to appreciate the worlds of art and literature. An excellent student, Lady Bird eventually made her way to the University of Texas in Austin, where she graduated at the top of her class with a degree in journalism.

In 1934, Lady Bird was introduced to Lyndon Johnson by a mutual friend, Eugene Lassiter. The following day, Lyndon proposed. She refused, and when he asked her again a few days later she said no once again. Johnson returned to Washington, D.C., but his pursuit of Lady Bird continued unabated. Two months later, he finally convinced her to accept his proposal and they were married on November 17, 1934. The nervous bridegroom reportedly forgot the ring and had to send a witness over to the local Sears, where the witness bought a three dollar gold band.

Lyndon's political career began to take off, and in 1937 he was elected as a Congressman from Texas. For the next 12 years, the Johnsons lived a typically busy lifestyle in Washington. Lady Bird helped out around the office and was LBJ's main sounding board. In 1942, Lady Bird invested some of her own money in a small radio station in Austin, Texas. 20 years later, under the guidance of Lady Bird's sage management, station KTBC was worth approximately seven million dollars.

Lady Bird suffered through four miscarriages before giving birth to Lynda Bird in March of 1944. Three years later she would give birth to her second and last daughter, Lucy Baines.

In 1948, Johnson was elected to the U.S. Senate, in part thanks to Lady Bird, who was extremely active throughout his campaign. Johnson quickly became the majority leader, and in 1960 he was chosen to be Kennedy's Vice President. The Johnson's years as the nation's Second Couple saw no let up in their social activities. They entertained dignitaries from around the world, both at the their home in Washington as well as at the LBJ ranch in Texas.

Despite the tragic circumstances with which Lady Bird became the First Lady, she undertook her new role with a great deal of zeal. She made herself far more available to the press than any First Lady had done in years, and reporters often looked to her when they needed a good quote to spice up a story. But Lady Bird made her presence felt in more important ways as well. She helped her husband fight the war on poverty by visiting depressed areas across the country, and instituted her own "Beautification Program," to convert environmentally decimated areas back to their original splendor.

When her husband ran for election in 1964, she once again campaigned on his behalf, making dozens of speeches and shaking thousands of hands. Her own whistle stop tour of the south was known as the "Lady Bird Special," and she compiled over fifteen hundred miles on the forty-seven-stop trip. After Johnson's election, Lady Bird began fighting for her major cause: conservation. The Highway Beautification Act of 1965 was also known as the "Lady Bird Act."

Upon retiring to their LBJ Ranch in Texas in 1969, the Johnsons remained active. They supervised the building of LBJ's presidential library, as well as a municipal park that was named after Lady Bird. In 1976, Lady Bird took part in the Salute to America program, and in 1988 she moved to Austin, Texas. She remains a supporter of the National Wildflower Research Center and serves on the Board of the National Geographic Society.

Thelma Catherine (Patricia) Ryan Nixon

Born: March 16, 1912
Died: June 22, 1993
First Lady: 1969-1974

In spite of the fact that she was born on March 16, Thelma Ryan's father — who did not hear of his daughter's birth until March 17th — insisted that she was a St. Patrick's Day baby, and thus bestowed the nickname Patricia upon her. The name stuck.

When Pat was two years old, her father moved the family from the small mining town of Ely, Nevada to a farm in Artesia, California. Growing up on a farm, Pat learned the value of hard work from an early age. When her mother died in 1925, Pat had to take over many new responsibilities in addition to her work around the farm. Most trying, perhaps, was the care of her father, who had developed silicosis from working in the Nevada mines.

After her father's death in 1929, Pat officially changed her name to Patricia in his honor. She then graduated from high school and moved to New York, where she found work in a hospital. After two years in the Big Apple, she returned to California and enrolled at USC, where she studied merchandising. Upon graduating, she passed on a career in merchandising in favor of a job teaching school in nearby Whittier. While living in Whittier, Pat became involved with a small community theater company. One day, a young lawyer named Richard Nixon tried out for, and was awarded, the romantic lead opposite Pat in a production of the Alexander Wollcott-George S. Kaufman play, *The Dark Tower*. The night after their first rehearsal together, the smitten Nixon proposed. Pat declined his offer and continued to date several other men who lived in town. Richard, however, was extremely patient; in fact, he often drove Pat to and from the dates she had with other men. Finally, in June of 1940, after two years of waiting, he got what he wanted — Pat Ryan became his wife.

Nixon's political career took them first to Washington and then to Iowa. They were separated briefly when Richard went to fight in the South Pacific during World War II and Pat took a job in San Francisco. Reunited at the close of 1944 in Whittier, the couple decided it was time to start a family, and in February, 1946, their first daughter, Tricia, was born. One month later, Richard defeated the incumbent and won a congressional seat. Pat played an important role in this campaign, practically running the office single-handedly.

The couple moved to Washington, and a year later Pat gave birth to their second daughter, Julie. In 1950, Nixon was elected to the U.S. Senate. Ten years later, he would become the nation's Vice President. During her eight years as the Second Lady, Pat assumed greater and greater responsibilities. By day she made public appearances as schools and hospitals; by night she entertained world leaders. She traveled everywhere with her husband, visiting more than 50 countries.

After their close defeat in the 1960 presidential election, the devastated Pat made Richard promise he would never run for office again. He agreed and the couple moved back to Los Angeles, where Richard resumed his private law practice. In less than a year, Richard announced his candidacy for Governor of California. Pat was incensed, but after the intervention of her daughters, she relented. Nixon lost this race too, however, and in 1963 the family moved to New York, where Richard joined a prestigious law firm and earned a large salary. During the next five years, the Nixons enjoyed the high life; it was the first time either of them had actually been wealthy.

Nixon entered the political arena once again in 1968, and he was swept into the highest office in the land. Because of the tremendous influence of Nixon's staff, Pat did not play a very large role in the White House. She hosted dinners and invited such great musicians as Duke Ellington, Isaac Stern, and Leonard Bernstein to perform at a variety of functions. She also spent as much as four hours a day personally answering the mail and redecorating the public rooms of the White House. Access to the White House for the disabled, blind and deaf was greatly improved because of the First Lady. Pat continued to travel extensively with

Richard, and even made a couple of solo trips as a good-will ambassador — to Peru to help accident victims in 1970 and to Africa to aid famine victims in 1972.

After Nixon's resignation, the couple returned to San Clemente, California. In 1976, Pat suffered a stroke, followed by another one seven years later. She passed away in 1993.

Elizabeth Bloomer Ford

Born: April 18, 1918
First Lady: 1974-1977

Betty Ford was born in Chicago, Illinois and raised in Grand Rapids, Michigan. As a child, she loved to dance, and would later become a dance teacher herself. Her father died when she was just 16 years old, and two years later Betty enrolled at the Bennington School of Dance in Vermont. While at Bennington, Betty met Martha Graham, and followed her back to New York where she studied dance under the legendary choreographer for two years. Betty also managed to do some modeling for the John Robert Powers Agency while living in the Big Apple.

Upon returning home, she married William

Warren in 1942. The marriage only lasted for five years, ending in divorce in 1947. That same year, Betty began dating former high school football star Gerald Ford. They were married nine months later, and the following month Ford was elected to the House of Representatives. The couple moved to Washington and would stay there for the next 28 years.

Life as a popular Congressman's wife was not easy for Betty. Gerald was out of town on business more often than he was home, and she had to raise their four children on her own. In addition, she no longer had the time to pursue her interest in dancing. It was a lonely time for Betty, and eventually led to a nervous breakdown.

When Ford was asked to take over the vice presidency in the wake of Spiro Agnew's resignation, Betty was thrust into the spotlight. She was immediately asked for her opinion on abortion, and when she responded with a pro-choice position, she angered a great many of her husband's supporters. Others, however, cheered her stance and her bravery for stating her position. The same was true of Betty's remark on *60 Minutes* that she wouldn't be surprised if her 18 year old daughter were sexually active.

Two months into her stint as the First Lady, Betty had to undergo a mastectomy. Her willingness to talk about the operation and about breast cancer inspired a flood of women to have their breasts examined, which undoubtedly saved many lives (including Marguerite (Happy) Rockefeller, wife of the Vice President, who had one of her breasts removed just weeks after Betty's operation). Betty's outspoken attitude probably marked her time as First Lady more than anything else. She was a champion of the Equal Rights Amendment, and encouraged Gerald to appoint women to important political positions.

After Ford lost his bid for the presidency in 1976, he and Betty retired to Palm Springs, California. In 1978, Betty went public with the news that she had a drug and alcohol problem. This openness led to the creation of the Betty Ford Center, where drug addicts and alcoholics could seek rehabilitation. She published her memoirs, *The Times of My Life*, in 1978, and a television movie about her was produced a few years later. In 1987, she published her second book, *Betty; A Glad Awakening*. She continues to live with Gerald in Palm Springs.

Rosalynn Smith Carter
Born: August 18, 1927
First Lady: 1977-1981

The desire to work extremely hard that Rosalynn Carter demonstrated during her years as the First Lady was a virtue that was instilled in her from childhood onwards. Rosalynn was 13 when her father died, and as the oldest of 4 children, she took on many additional responsibilities around the house. At the age of 15, she helped out financially with the money she earned at a beauty shop in her hometown of Plains, Georgia. When she graduated from Plains High School in 1944, she was the class valedictorian.

In 1945, Jimmy Carter, visiting Plains while on leave from the U.S. Naval Academy at Annapolis, Maryland, began to take notice of his sister's girlfriend. One year later, Jimmy and Rosalynn were married.

Rosalynn had always wanted to break free of the small town where she had been born and raised, and with Jimmy her dreams came true. As a naval officer, he was stationed at various points around the world, and she went with him everywhere. They lived in New York, Connecticut, and Hawaii. During this period, Rosalynn gave birth to three sons. But when

Jimmy's father passed away, Jimmy decided to quit his naval career and return to Plains to run his father's peanut business. Rosalynn was not happy about the prospect of returning to the town she had so desperately sought to leave, but she made the best of things and even began to take an active interest in the day-to-day running of the family business. When Jimmy started to get involved in politics, Rosalynn took over the peanut farm and successfully ran the whole operation.

In 1967, at the age of 40, Rosalynn gave birth to a daughter, Amy. Two years later, Jimmy was elected as the Governor of Georgia. Rosalynn did not relish such traditional duties of the First Lady of Georgia as entertaining and meeting the public. Instead, she set to work improving the services which were available to the handicapped, volunteered at area hospitals, and was a vocal supporter of the ERA. She was appointed to the Governor's Commission to Improve Services for the Mentally and Emotionally Handicapped, and made a point of visiting every mental health facility in Georgia. Rosalynn was also the honorary chairperson of Georgia's Special Olympics.

By the time Carter was ready to campaign for the presidency, Rosalynn was truly one of his most important advisors. She campaigned right alongside of him, helped him with his speeches, and offered advice on a wide variety of subjects. Upon entering the White House, Rosalynn wasted no time getting busy. She traveled around the world, attended hours and hours of important meetings (including cabinet meetings), sat in on briefing sessions, worked with the mentally ill, and organized dozens of formal dinners and receptions for such dignitaries as President Anwar Sadat, Prime Minister Menacham Begin, and Soviet premier Leonid Brezhnev. Her testimony in front of a Senate committee on mental health legislation was only the second time a First Lady had ever made such an appearance. Perhaps only Eleanor Roosevelt and Abigail Adams have ever done so much as First Ladies.

After Carter's defeat in 1979, he and Rosalynn returned to Plains, where they continued to channel their energies into working with the poor, the disabled, and the disenfranchised. One of their most progressive programs is Habitat for Humanity, in which volunteers build homes for those who otherwise could not afford them. Another noteworthy organization is the Friendship Force, which promotes friendship around the world. The couple's generous work continues to this day.

Nancy Davis Reagan

Born: July 6, 1921
First Lady: 1981-1989

Nancy was actually born Anne Frances Robbins. Her father, Kenneth Robbins, left her and her mother soon after she was born. Over the next six years, Anne lived with relatives in Baltimore while her mother, an actress, was on tour with a theater company. When Anne was eight years old, her mother married Dr. Loyal Davis, and Anne permanently began using the nickname Nancy that her mother often used for her. When she turned 14, Nancy would also take the last name of her step-father when he officially adopted her.

Life with Dr. Davis was quite different than anything Nancy had known up until that point. Money was now abundant, and Nancy even had a coming out party at Chicago's Casino Club. After graduating from Smith College, Nancy began her acting career. It started with bit parts on Broadway, but when she signed a contract with MGM in 1949, she became a busy working actress. She made several films in which she played the girl-next-door, and received her first starring role in *East Side, West Side*. She met Ronald Reagan in 1949 when he was president of the Screen Actors Guild, and Nancy was concerned about receiving Communist propaganda in a time when the Red Scare was taking place in Hollywood. Ronald and Nancy were married three years later; actor William Holden was the best man. Nancy's final film performance came in 1957, when she co-starred with Ronald in *Hellcats of the Navy*.

Reagan won election as the Governor of California in 1966. As the First Lady of California, Nancy was often criticized for being exceedingly demanding on both her husband and the members of their household staff. The public also rebuked her for refusing to socialize with anybody but Hollywood stars and such members of the upper class as Betsy Bloomingdale and Lee Annenberg. Such criticisms would follow her straight to the White House.

During her first year in the White House, feminists were outraged by her opposition to the ERA, and she angered the general public by spending outrageous amounts of money on the inaugural ball, clothing, and new china for the White House in a time when everyone was trying to make sacrifices for the sake of the sickly economy.

But after this disastrous beginning, Nancy found something to latch onto which would give her a dose of credibility: the anti-drug movement. She began to speak to children and recovering drug addicts, and instituted the

"Just Say No" campaign. Her other forte', of course, was entertaining. Nancy brought back the white tie and tails affair, formal gowns, expensive jewelry, and hosted many formal receptions for dignitaries from around the world.

It may never be known exactly how much power Nancy had during her tenure as First Lady. Towards the end of Reagan's term, it has been suggested that Nancy fired several key presidential aides, and that she often put words into Ronald's mouth. For these actions, she earned the nickname "Dragon Lady."

When the Reagan's time in the White House came to an end, they retired to Bel Air, California. Nancy published her autobiography, *My Turn*, in 1989, and she continues to be active in the fight against drug abuse. Nancy also became a member of the Board of Directors of Revlon Corporation in 1989.

Barbara Pierce Bush

Born: June 8, 1924
First Lady: 1989-1993

Barbara Bush is the daughter of the *McCalls/ Redbook* publisher Marvin Pierce. She was raised in the suburban town of Rye, New York, and attended boarding school at Ashley Hall in South Carolina. One day, when she was 16 years old, she attended a dance at the Round Hill Country Club in Greenwich, Connecticut, and met George Bush, who was, at the time, a senior at Phillips Academy in Andover, Massachusetts. They were engaged in August of 1943, just before George took off for the South Pacific, where he served as a pilot (all of his planes were named "Barbara"). Barbara enrolled at Smith College for women, where she became captain of the freshman soccer team. She eventually dropped out of college, and shortly after George returned from the War, the couple was married.

After moving from Michigan to Maine and then to Virginia while George trained new pilots, the newlyweds settled down in New Haven, Connecticut, where George attended Yale University and where Barbara gave birth to the first of six children. The couple eventually put their roots down in Texas, and George became a success in the oil industry. Turning to politics, Bush continued his winning ways. But his appointments to a wide variety of positions also meant that Barbara had to organize many, many moves — 29 in 44 years! 18 cities in all!

After her daughter Robin's death from leukemia at the tender age of four (a traumatic experience that is supposedly the reason for the color of Barbara's hair), Barbara became actively involved in providing support for those suffering from illness and disease, a practice she continues today. Among the foundations for which she has donated her time are the Leukemia Society of America and the March of Dimes. Likewise, when it became apparent that her son Neil was dyslexic, she became a promoter of literacy in America, and established the Barbara Bush Foundation for Family Literacy. This foundation looks to the role of the family in overcoming literacy problems.

One of the high points of Barbara's life was the time she spent in China while her husband was working in Beijing as the head of the United States Liaison Office. Barbara loved the people and culture of China, and spent a great deal of her time studying Chinese, learning Tai Chi, and bicycling.

As First Lady, she continued to devote her time to a variety of social causes, from AIDS to the homeless to educating our nation's children. In the wake of her term as First Lady, she continues her social work as well as finding time to host family gatherings for her five children and eleven grandchildren.

Hillary Rodham Clinton

Born: October 26, 1947
First Lady: 1993-

Hillary Rodham Clinton was born on the North Side of Chicago, Illinois, and raised in nearby Park Ridge. Her father, Hugh E. Rodham, owned a textile business, and her mother, Dorothy, stayed at home and raised Hillary and her two brothers. Hillary's parents were Methodists, and the present First Lady had a strong religious upbringing.

Hugh Rodham's college education enabled him to escape a life spent in the coal mines, and he was committed to seeing that his children would work hard in school and follow in his steps by graduating college. Dorothy Rodham, who had not gone to college but who was continually taking a variety of college courses throughout Hillary's childhood, felt as strongly as her husband did about the value of a college education.

By all accounts, Hillary's childhood was like something out of an *Ozzie and Harriet* episode. She spent her winters playing with neighborhood children in the snow, and her summers bicycling through the safe streets of her neighborhood. Hillary eventually graduated in the top five percent of her class at Maine South

High School.

The Kennedy assassination and attending a speech given by Martin Luther King, Jr. had a profound effect on Hillary in the early 1960s, and pushed her growing interest in politics to the point of near-obsession. She enrolled in Wellsley College in 1965 and began volunteering for the Republican party, especially for the campaign of Massachusetts Attorney General Edward Brooke, who was running for the U.S. Senate.

As the sixties marched onward, Hillary's political views gradually shifted to the left. In 1968, she began to feel that such Republicans as Barry Goldwater were not effectively dealing with the reality of the situation on the streets of America. Making the switch, she began working for liberal Eugene McCarthy. She also began marching for civil rights and protesting the war in Vietnam. In her junior year of college, Hillary was elected president of the student government.

In early 1971, while attending Yale Law School, Hillary met Bill Clinton. Their first meeting occurred in the library. Bill, who was also attending Yale, couldn't take his eyes off of Hillary. After growing tired of his obvious staring, Hillary finally approached him and insisted that he introduce himself. They fell in love and by Fall of that same year they had moved in together.

After working for the failed George McGovern presidential campaign, Bill and Hillary returned to Yale and completed their education. When she was 26, Hillary was one of a hand-picked group of young lawyers who worked behind-the-scenes on the Watergate investigation. Despite the fact that Hillary was in Washington and Bill had headed back to Little Rock, the two kept in constant touch and even managed to visit each other on occasion. When Nixon resigned, Hillary made one of the biggest decisions of her life: she passed on several important job opportunities so that she could join Bill in Arkansas. She accepted a job teaching at the University of Arkansas Law School (where Bill was also teaching) and headed south. They were married on October 11, 1975.

In 1976, Hillary left Arkansas to work for Jimmy Carter's presidential campaign. During this period, Bill Clinton won election as Arkansas' Attorney General. Hillary then accepted a job with a Little Rock law firm. She helped found the Arkansas Advocates for Children and Families, and became more and more involved in the rights of children.

Bill was elected as the Governor of Arkansas in 1978; one year later, Hillary was promoted to a partner in the law firm she had joined just a few years earlier. In February of 1980, Hillary gave birth to their one and only child, Chelsea. Dividing her time between being the state's First Lady and her duties with the law firm and motherhood was no easy task. But Hillary managed to do it all, even finding time to chair Arkansas' Education Standards Committee among myriad social projects with which she became involved.

After Bill Clinton's election as President of the United States in 1992, Hillary continued her long involvement in a variety of social issues. At the top of the list has been the nation's health care system; President Clinton named her the chairman of the Presidential Task Force on National Health Care Reform. But she has also remained deeply involved in issues surrounding education, the family, and children's rights. By the time her tenure as First Lady comes to a close, there seems to be a good chance that Hillary Rodham Clinton will stand with Abigail Adams, Eleanor Roosevelt, and Rosalynn Carter as the most influential women to ever inhabit the White House.